THE HOUSE
AT
OTOWI BRIDGE

*The Story of Edith Warner
and Los Alamos*

PEGGY POND CHURCH

COMPOSED, PRINTED AND BOUND
AT THE UNIVERSITY OF NEW MEXICO PRINTING PLANT
ALBUQUERQUE, NEW MEXICO, U.S.A.
LIBRARY OF CONGRESS CATALOG CARD NUMBER 60-13408
Clothbound ISBN 0-8263-0014-6
Paperbound ISBN 0-8263-0281-5
Tenth paperbound printing,
University of New Mexico Press, 1990

TO DOROTHY McKIBBIN

FOR THE SAKE OF THE OLD TIMES AND THE NEW

CONTENTS

ACKNOWLEDGMENTS

GRATEFUL acknowledgement is made to Dr. J. Robert Oppenheimer for permission to quote from *Science and the Common Understanding;* to the *New York Times* for quotations from an article by Bill Becker on Niels Bohr; to The American Council for Nationalities Service for use of portions of my article, "Winter Feast," previously published in *Common Ground,* and to *Neighborhood: A Settlement Quarterly,* for Edith Warner's essay on her Pueblo neighbors.

I am especially indebted to Velma Warner Ludlow for the material she entrusted to my care and for the faith and patience with which she has awaited the outcome; to Peter (Mrs. C. Earle) Miller for her letters which did so much to set the tone of the book; to Dr. Philip Morrison for the use of his letter; and to Mrs. L. D. P. King who made possible an unforgettable evening of reminiscence among Edith Warner's friends at Los Alamos.

I owe more than I can say to May Sarton for her severe and loving criticism of the first draft, to Erna Fergusson for her appreciation of the second, and above all to Roland Dickey for his perceptive eye and the valiant use of his editorial scissors.

—PEGGY POND CHURCH

I HAVE BEEN sitting in my garden this morning thinking of Edith Warner, how many years it has been since she died and how fast the world we knew has gone on changing. She lies in an Indian grave near the Pueblo of San Ildefonso, nothing over her but the earth hard as a bare heel, and the fragments of the clay pots that were broken over the grave according to the ancient custom of the Pueblos. The little house she lived in beside the bridge was already falling to pieces when I saw it last. The new bridge of towering rigid steel, with two lanes for the traffic that now speeds back and forth to Los Alamos, crosses the Rio Grande close to the wellhouse. The vines that used to hang there, their leaves so glossy and cool in the quivery summer heat, are a mass of clotted dry stems and tendrils. I suppose hardly anyone stops to listen to the river any more.

But I still see Edith standing in the doorway, her thin figure straight as an aspen in a mountain forest, her eyes lifted to the long dark rim of the mesa east of the river. She watches the sky for the northward flight of the wild geese, "that long silver V endlessly circling and reforming," to tell us of spring's sure return. The brown buckskin moccasins in which she moved so quietly about her busy days are lapped over at the ankles and fastened in the Navajo style with a silver button—the only concession to Indian costume she ever made. In memory I still see the worn scrubbed boards of the kitchen floor behind her, the old-fashioned range with its twin warming ovens and the woodbox near it that Tilano kept filled with sticks of knotted juniper. The copper kettle simmers on the stove and the house is filled with the warm smell of baking bread.

Old Tilano, who was nearly sixty when he came across the bridge from the pueblo to live with Edith at "the place where the river

makes a noise," comes in from the well and smiles as he sets the bucket of water beside the kitchen door. I shall never forget the gentleness and dignity of his face, brown as a weathered rock, the two black braids of his hair wound with yarn as blue as the sky at midday. I have a picture of him which has stood for a long time on my desk. Dressed in jeans, a sun-faded shirt, a wrinkled cowboy hat, he is stooping to pour clean water over the bare feet of my small son, muddy with play at the edge of the muddy river. The little boy has grown to manhood and has children of his own. Tilano has lived out his life and gone, like Edith, to be part of the timeless spirit of the land.

On the high Pajarito Plateau west of the river, where as a child I used to hunt for arrowheads among the pueblo ruins, the city of Los Alamos now sprawls with its fierce and guarded laboratories, its rows of modern houses, its theaters and flashy supermarkets. The paved road that runs from north to south across the plateau parallels the remnants of an old trail worn ankle-deep in places by the moccasined feet of Indians. On one side of the road is a tightly woven metal fence bearing in enormous red letters the warning DANGER! PELIGROSO! On the other, a "sacred area" has been set aside where the Indians of San Ildefonso still tend traditional shrines and place prayer plumes when their hearts are right.

The Pajarito Plateau opens like a huge fan from an arc of blue mountains in northwestern New Mexico. From a distance it looks almost level, covered with a dark blanket of yellow pine. It is grooved by canyons that radiate from the mountains like the crudely drawn spokes of a wheel. The canyon walls rise through many-colored layers of hardened volcanic ash, pink and rose and buff, like petrified waves. Some of the ridges between the canyons are narrow, rounded like tongues or sleeping lizards. Others are wide and flat, dotted with the mounds of pre-Columbian Indian villages and a few cultivated fields where Spanish-American families used to raise scanty patches of beans in summer, returning in winter to their adobe homes along the Rio Grande.

During the centuries of the Crusades in Europe, the time of the great khans in Asia, through the days when Columbus struggled for ships and money to sail west to the Orient, Indians were living in

settled communities among these canyons and mesas. When the Spaniards came in the sixteenth century they found the villages deserted. The dwellings had fallen into mounds of stone. The sacred kivas were open to the sun and rain. No one knew what had become of the ancient inhabitants. Perhaps drought drove them away. Perhaps they felt their gods had failed them, or that they had failed their gods. Some of the Indians living along the Rio Grande claim them as their ancestors, but no one has been able to make the broken pieces of the puzzle fit together.

A few years ago, returning for a nostalgic visit to scenes of my own childhood, I slept for a night on the ground below Tsirege, one of the largest of the ancient villages. The word means Place of the Bird People. Carried over into Spanish as Pajarito, "little bird," it became the name by which the whole plateau is known. Long ago, for two magic years, my restless father managed a dude-ranch in Pajarito Canyon, two miles above the now-forbidding fence. When I was a child of twelve I used to ride my barebacked horse to Tsirege and spend hours wondering about the vanished people who had chosen to build their homes in situations of such extraordinary beauty. I remember nothing so still as the silence around that mesa. Eagles soared without sound in the blue above it. Lizards moved in a whisper among the fallen housewalls. Now as I slept and woke and looked up at the turning patterns of the stars, I could hear through the earth the hum of great dynamos that I knew had to do with modern man's purpose of destruction. I remembered a handful of childish treasures I had hidden at the roots of an old tree in the canyon and knew that I could never go back again to find them.

It was drought that forced us to leave the Pajarito at the end of the second summer. The little stream we used to wade in failed and the spring from which our water had been piped dried up. I remember how we children cried as we drove away, turning for long last looks at the caves where we had played and roasted apples, at our secret hiding places among the cliffs, and the fields where we had chased our stubborn horses.

Almost thirty years later I was exiled from the plateau for the second time when the boys' school my father founded and in which my husband taught for twenty years was taken over by the Govern-

ment, along with several thousand acres of surrounding plateau and mountain land, for the top-secret project which was working to develop the atomic bomb. The school was called Los Alamos after the deep canyon which bordered the mesa to the south and which was groved with cottonwood trees along the sandy trickle of its stream. It was a name that no one suspected would one day be famous throughout the world.

It was Edith Warner in her little house by the bridge on the road to Los Alamos, who saw it all happen. Through the years of upheaval she and Tilano guarded for us all the changeless essence. In 1943 she began the series of remarkable Christmas letters which kept the land alive for those of us in exile. She wrote us the news of plowing and planting, of the anguish of dust and wind, the blessing of rainfall, pine knots gathered each autumn, the ancient Indian rituals continued even while the sound of experimental blasts from the mesas gave notice that a new and threatening age had come upon us. It brought us a feeling of calm to know she was still there. It was as though we still had a little corner of the Pajarito land we could call our own. She kept watch for us all over the circling seasons and listened for us to the music of the river.

This shy little spinster from Pennsylvania lived for more than twenty years as neighbor to the Indians of San Ildefonso Pueblo, and when she died they buried her among them. Through the Indians she was in touch with a wisdom that has been almost forgotten. The scientists who took our place at Los Alamos became her friends. It was one of the strange aspects of Edith Warner's fate that brought these men and their wives from many nations to gather around her table. Among them were some of the great minds in Europe and America, and their work was to change our world beyond believing. Edith's house became a kind of sanctuary for them in the tense years before Hiroshima. When the new bridge brought the road to Los Alamos so close to the house that life there could no longer be endured, some of the same men whose minds conceived the atomic bomb worked side by side with the Indians to build a new house for Edith and Tilano. When Edith died, Niels Bohr, great physicist, and also, as she tells us, a great man, wrote her sister: "The memory of Edith Warner, a noble personality, and of the

enchanting environment in which she lived, will always be cherished by everyone who met her. Although, in the days of the war it was not possible to speak freely about the hopes and anxieties in one's mind, I felt that your sister had an intuitive understanding which was a bond between us."

Many of us hoped that Edith would someday be able to write her story. She made an attempt, but after the first few pages it sounded to her too much like the standard adventure: "White woman moves West. Lives among Indians." Better nothing than that, she thought, and gave it up. She found herself unable to speak of her deep friendship with her Indian neighbors. I remember what a dislike she had, really the only sharp animosity I ever heard her express, for the anthropologists who kept intruding in the village, prying like irreverent children into the secrets of the kiva. In all her years at the bridge she allowed herself to learn only a few playful words of Tewa because she wanted the village people to keep, even from her, the privacy of their language. She never asked an Indian what his ceremonies "meant" any more than she ever asked me the meaning of the poems I showed her, knowing that the ritual, like the poem, must be its own communication. Besides the unfinished manuscript and the handful of Christmas letters, a few typed pages of her journal are all Edith felt willing to leave behind in writing.

"This is the story of a house," her manuscript begins, "a house that stood for many years beside a bridge between two worlds." It stood, too, in the shadow of Los Alamos, the mushrooming shadow of violent change in which all of us now must go on living. More than the story of a house, it is the story of a woman who out of almost nothing made an oasis of serenity and beauty in a world that seemed to grow every day more threatening. Edith Warner died in 1951, her roots still deep and unshaken. The sound of the river was with her to the end.

Because the little house and its rebuilding had meaning for so many, because Edith and Tilano still live as part of my own inner world, I try now to join the broken threads of her story together and weave them with my own.

ONE

MY FATHER, Ashley Pond, grew up in Detroit, a delicate boy who suffered through his school days and even through college with bronchitis. He never forgot the dreary weeks spent in boarding school infirmaries, the choking grey skies, the ominous report cards with their toll of missed classes and failing grades. He was the only surviving son of a brilliant man and carried the burden of his father's disappointment through his boyhood.

During the Spanish-American War he enlisted with Roosevelt's Rough Riders, but before he saw active duty a siege of typhoid nearly finished him. His father sent him West to recover his health —a custom which was becoming increasingly prevalent at that time. He lived for months with cattle ranchers on the eastern slope of the Rockies, riding horseback all day long, cooking his meals over campfires, sleeping often under the stars. It was the kind of life, he came to feel, for which men had been made. He began to dream of a school where city boys from wealthy families like his own could regain their heritage of outdoor wisdom at the same time that they were being prepared for college and the responsibilities which their position in life demanded. He was convinced that hours spent on the trail with a knowledgeable cowpony would teach a boy more that he needed to know as a man, than he could ever learn from textbooks.

In the autumn of 1904 his dream was about to be realized. The year before he had met and married a lively girl who came out from St. Louis to spend the summers on her grandfather's ranch near Watrous in Mora County, New Mexico. A few miles away, in Shoemaker Canyon where the Santa Fe Railroad still runs, he found a site for his school that pleased him. Buildings were ready.

A staff had been engaged. One night, after weeks of unseasonal rains, a railway embankment near the ranch gave way and released tons of flooding water from the swollen Mora River. He had barely time to carry his wife, and the ten-months-old infant who was myself, to a barn on higher ground. Everything he owned was washed away. Adobe buildings dissolved into mud. Navajo rugs were buried in cornfields. An enormous hotel-sized icebox never has been found. It was years before he was financially able to start again.

After a few years back in Michigan, where he entered business, and where my brother and sister both were born—worse luck for them, I always boasted—his father died and left him with an independent income. He returned at once to New Mexico and began years of search for a place to start his school again.

Through an archaeologist friend in Santa Fe he became interested in the Pajarito Plateau. The dude ranch venture in Pajarito Canyon was only intended to be temporary. Soon after it failed he managed to acquire a piece of property on one of the highest mesas to the north. It looked ideal for the school he had never ceased to dream of. A man named Brook had homesteaded the place and put up a few ramshackle buildings near a rain-fed and muddy pool where ducks swam. There were several acres of cultivated fields. The mesa rose high above the barren and broken hills of the Rio Grande Valley, safely above the reach of any flood. The Jemez Mountains were only a mile or two away and the Sangre de Cristos ran the whole length of the eastern horizon into Colorado. A more isolated spot could hardly be imagined, but isolation was an important part of my father's plan.

A two-story log building was put up, with kitchen and common room and classrooms on the first floor, bedrooms and sleeping porches above. The school opened in 1917. From the beginning it was a self-contained community with its own commissary, electric light-plant and machine shops. Each boy was assigned his own horse to ride. Hay from the fields was stored in a huge barn. Silos for grain were built, corrals and saddlerooms constructed. The duck pond was enlarged and a storage house built beside it to hold the year's supply of ice that was cut each winter. Water was pumped from a stream in a nearby canyon and stored in a big tank that stood

on stilts near the mound of the small ruin in back of the main building.

Soon after the school was established my father withdrew from active participation in its affairs and retired to make his home in Santa Fe. He was a man of vision rather than an educator and had the wisdom to leave it to those more qualified than himself to carry out his dream. To run his school he selected A. J. Connell, who had been active in the Boy Scout movement and who was for many years a ranger in the United States Forest Service. Under Connell's direction the school grew from a student body of one in its first year to a capacity enrollment of forty-four. In December of 1942 the Government took over the property by process of condemnation for the Manhattan Project, and the history of Los Alamos School abruptly ended. I have always been glad that my father, who died in 1933, did not live to see the day.

In 1924 I married Fermor Church, one of the young men who came out from New England to teach at Los Alamos, and I went there to live, the first faculty wife to join that small and secluded community. I was rather pleased with myself for having outwitted my father who had been so unfeeling as to plan his school for boys and not for girls. I had his own love of horses and mountain trails, and years of Eastern boarding school and college had not cured me.

In those first years I had glamorous ideas of ranch-life. For our honeymoon my husband took me to the mountain cabin where the boys often went on week-end packtrips. It was set among quaking aspens at the head of a steep valley. The birds had the world to themselves, and the call of the towhee was like a string of jewels let down among the dark branches of the fir trees. When the chores were done each day we would saddle up our horses. I had been taught to curry and brush my horse before I was eight, and I proudly placed the striped Navajo blanket on her back just so, the crease at her withers and the two sides even, and swung into place the heavy western saddle that had belonged to my grandfather. The mare would draw in a deep breath while I pulled the front cinch tight. We would tie a canteen to each of the saddles and place a sandwich lunch in the saddlebags. I wore spurs that were not so much to goad my willing mare as to control her, a Stetson hat like

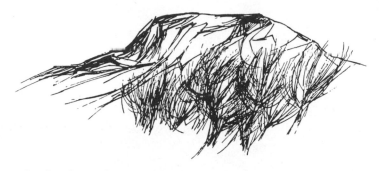

my husband's, and a pair of leather chaps to protect my knees when our trail led through heavy brush or low-limbed fir trees. We would ride at a walk or a slow trot all day, sometimes to the grassy top of a mountain where a mound of stones marked an old Indian shrine, sometimes to the wide treeless valley that was part of an extinct crater, filled now with flocks of grazing sheep and cattle.

At evening we returned to our cabin to unsaddle the sweaty horses and watch them roll before we turned them loose to graze. I would struggle with the cast-iron Dutch ovens and the task of boiling beans or potatoes at an altitude of nine thousand feet, or take the easy way out and open a can of soup or tomatoes. I learned that to make boiled coffee was a special art. It must be taken from the fire at just the right time and settled with just the right amount of cold water. We drank it from big aluminum cups that burned our lips, but it tasted better than ambrosia.

My husband taught me, as the school boys on their week-end rides were carefully taught, to build a campfire. The best wood was juniper or oak that made long-lasting coals. The aspen and fir in the mountains burned too quickly, but we made it do, letting it roar into its first great blaze and then die down to a mound of sparks before we placed our kettles on it. The mountains would grow dark around us while we ate by the light of a log placed at the back of the fire. Strange crashings of twigs out of the darkness would startle us. The horses whinnied now and then, and we could hear sheep bleating from some herder's lonely camp.

This was only a taste of the adventure that the boys of Los Alamos were permitted to experience on many of their spring and autumn weekends. They were taught the skills of outdoor living, the care

of themselves and their horses on the trail as thoroughly as the Latin and geometry that their college preparation demanded. When school was in session my husband was seldom able to ride with me. I was never allowed to ride with the boys, so I did my own exploring. There was no trail within seven miles of the school in any direction that I did not know. Even after my first son was born I used to leave him sleeping in his crib while I wandered as far as the time between bottle feedings allowed me.

Mr. Connell looked on my exploits with disapproval. The trouble with me, he said, was that I had not enough to keep me busy—and this judgment I used to deny with considerable temper. He would argue that modern life was spoiling women with its electricity and washing machines and vacuum cleaners. He always declared that the first thing the school had to do for a boy was undo the work of women. I got no credit at all for being resourceful in the woods, or being able to mend a broken tire chain with a strand of wire from some handy fencepost. Why, he wondered inconsistently, couldn't I sit placidly knitting baby booties like the nurse in her spare time instead of forever fretting my husband to companion me on all-day picnics?

For a long time the nurse at the school was my only woman companion, and she had her own routine that kept her busy. The thirty-five mile drive to Santa Fe used to take more than three hours and we had to cross arroyos often treacherous with sand or angry with flashing water. There was only a narrow railway trestle over the Rio Grande at the place we called Otowi, and we drove across straddling the rails on the open ties with the earth-colored water coiling underneath as muscular as a snake. I remember the first Christmas when we were planning to spend the day with my parents in Santa Fe, we woke to find the world covered with three feet of snow, and had to inch our way down the steep switchback road behind a snowplow.

Needless to say, we left the mesa very seldom. Our nearest neighbors were the Smithwicks, who looked after a mentally retarded boy, at Anchor Ranch five miles to the south. When I grew hungry for female gossip I would put sandwiches in my saddlebags and ride over to spend the day with Connie Smithwick.

It was there on an autumn afternoon in 1925 that I first met Edith Warner. I remember her then as a shy and diffident person who wandered into the rustic sitting room while Connie and I were having tea. Where had this prim little figure come from, I wondered? She was wearing a blouse and skirt that looked as though they might have come out of a missionary barrel. I was not surprised when Connie told me later that "Miss Warner" had grown up as the eldest of five daughters in a Baptist minister's household in Pennsylvania. Toward the end of 1921 she suffered some kind of breakdown, and a wise diagnostician, finding no physical cause for her persistent illness, prescribed a year of outdoor life without responsibilities. Almost at random she had chosen to spend that year of freedom in New Mexico. A friend of hers had been there and recommended a small guest ranch in Frijoles Canyon west of Santa Fe. At the end of her year Edith Warner had fallen in love with the country and decided she could live happily no place else. Since then, in spite of her delicate health, she had been trying one expedient after another to earn a living so she would not have to return to the clouded and crowded atmosphere of Pennsylvania. The Smithwicks who had met Edith during her first year in New Mexico, had taken a liking to her and asked her to live with them awhile as a kind of governess to the young boy in their care.

Miss Warner took almost no part in the conversation that afternoon except to show a city-dweller's sentimental enthusiasm for wildflowers. She was narrow-shouldered and the bones in her face showed too plainly. Her eyes were guarded by wide-rimmed glasses and she wore her hair coiled limply as though she had long ago given up the effort to be pretty. It seemed to me that no one could belong less to this land of burning skies and mountains. What was there about this landscape that attracted her, I wondered? I had the born Westerner's easy scorn for the tenderfoot and was sure this one would not last long.

How astonished I was to learn some three years later that Mr. Connell had given Miss Warner the job of looking after the freight at the little boxcar railway station beside the bridge at Otowi, and that, of all things, she was planning to open a tearoom.

TWO

EDITH WARNER was thirty years old when she left Pennsylvania in the fall of 1922. This was almost exactly the midpoint of her life. All of her future lay folded still within her, like the Mariposa lilies she came to love—those three-petaled white blossoms with the golden centers whose seed must often wait patiently through years of drought for enough moisture to make them germinate.

She had always been a serious child, her sister tells me, and until she was seven years old, the only one. Her first years were spent almost entirely with adults, of whom a grandfather had been especially close. On her mother's side she was German, on her father's English, Scotch and Welsh. Her father already had a young family when he gave up a career in business to enter the ministry. This sudden change of vocation took real courage. Because of his shyness, he found preaching difficult. Only stubborn determination, much like Edith herself showed later, and a deep religious conviction enabled him to persist in it. Her mother was a dynamic woman in whom gentleness and humility were blended with tremendous pride and strength of will. She had a gift for understanding people that was almost psychic. The German-Lutheran grandmother was a diminutive lady whose God was indeed a mighty fortress. She mixed her Biblical quotations with a sparkling sense of humor.

With such a background it was inevitable that the eldest daughter should grow up with a strong sense of duty. Edith was ten years old at the time her father entered the ministry and a large share of responsibility for helping with the busy household fell upon her shoulders. She became self-supporting as early as she could, as much to help with the financial burden as for her own sake. She was eighteen when she graduated from Normal school and began to

teach. She started out in a one-room country school where she handled all the subjects. Later she taught English in a high school in Philadelphia. She found this work desperately uncongenial. Looking back in the second year of her life beside the Rio Grande, she writes in her journal:

I have been lying here looking out at the mesa and the aspen all golden on the Sangres, and I know that no wooded, verdant country could make me feel as this one does. Its very nudity makes it intimate. There are only shadows to cover its bareness, and the snow that lies white in the spring. I think I could not bear again great masses of growing things. . . . It would stifle me as buildings do.

She worked for a while as industrial secretary for the Y.W.C.A. in Easton, Pennsylvania. This suited her a good deal better. It involved a lot of outdoor life, camping and picnicking with young working girls, which she enjoyed. In spite of her shyness she showed, like her mother, a real talent for working with people. She fell in love now and again during these years but none of the affairs materialized. Underneath her conscious duty-fulfilling will something was struggling to break forth into another kind of life. Perhaps her spirit belonged to the gods from the beginning as the eagles belong to the sky—the eagles in whose presence she says she could never feel anything but deep awe. Like a captive bird she was torn by the instinct to seek her freedom, though her mind was for a long time unaware of what she fought for. It was not long after the end of the First World War that her body, unable to stand the strain, rebelled.

"Perhaps the war and post-war years had been too strenuous," she said. "Perhaps unknown forces were changing the pattern of my life."

Afterwards it seemed important to her that everything happened almost without her own volition. It was the merest chance that she decided to go to New Mexico. She knew nothing about it. It was little more to her than a name in geography. The solitude and peace of the guest ranch in Frijoles Canyon sounded like heaven when her friend described it. She made ready, as though in a dream, for the long journey.

On an autumn evening in 1922, Edith Warner found herself on the station platform at Lamy waiting for the local train that would take her the eighteen remaining miles to Santa Fe. Darkness hid New Mexico. All around were the dark shapes of hills, their outlines sharp as knives against the bright black night. The stars seemed unbelievably close and brilliant. The crisp air was like nothing she had ever breathed. She began to feel that she had entered another world.

From Santa Fe the next morning she was driven forty miles to Frijoles. Mountains rimmed the world. The sky was as blue as though made of crystal. To the east the Sangre de Cristo Mountains shone with what seemed masses of molten metal far up their sides. Westward, patches of aspen splashed the same color along dark green slopes. The sand of the dry riverbeds shone golden. Rabbit brush, with its borrowed and beautiful Spanish name, "chamisa," bore lemon yellow blossoms above the golden green of its foliage.

The driver of the battered-looking automobile was John Boyd, who with his wife, Martha, was running the Frijoles guest ranch that year. He was a lanky Hoosier with picturesque mustaches and a pipe which he kept forever lighting. His sense of humor and his incomparable gift for storytelling had endeared him to the Indians who lived along the Rio Grande. They would laugh when he teased them, and share their stories with him. He was as full of Indian lore as a piñon tree is full of ripened cones in the season of harvest, when one has only to spread a cloth and shake the branches to bring the brown nuts raining down. Edith felt, as one of her letters tells us later, that it was John Boyd who really gave her the necessary background for understanding the Pueblo people.

Had I not come in that year of 1922 while the Boyds were at Frijoles, someone else might have lived in the house at Otowi bridge. Had they not taken me into their hearts I might never have known the people of San Ildefonso. Without Father Boyd's tutelage there could have been no background of understanding. It was he who taught me to watch for tracks on the trail, showed me the significance a stone might have.

On this first day, his conversation flowed over Edith like a wind. She found the breadth of landscape almost overwhelming. For miles stony hillsides alternated with sandy washes. In places the road seemed scarcely more than two faint tracks. Elsewhere the two tracks were deep ruts which had to be straddled gingerly as though the car were crossing a tightrope. After many miles the road suddenly steepened and dropped downward toward a river that split the bare landscape like a copper wire. This, John Boyd told Edith, was the Rio Grande. The river emerges at this point from behind the bulk of an iron-colored mesa, flattens out below the light, bright hills, then narrows and disappears again into a dark gorge. Westward beyond the river rises a fortress-like plateau, wall upon serrated wall of many-colored rock. The river guards its base like an ancient moat. I myself can never drive toward the Pajarito mesas without feeling what I did as a little girl, that I am about to enter a legendary land.

The road in those days crossed the river several miles south of Otowi over a battered and shaky wooden bridge at a railway siding called Buckman. It almost disappeared in a waste of sand, then suddenly turned and flung itself upward across the sloping surface of the plateau wall, upward and up while the river narrowed to a shimmering thread bordered by purple rocks and thin webs of green. Edith Warner could see again the Sangre de Cristos rising blue out of a basin of rosy hills. It seemed as though the sky were both above her and below.

After reaching the top of the plateau, the road twined for a while among almost level mesas and low broken cliffs. It zigzagged south across a series of steep canyons whose walls rose steplike in masses of gray and rose. The plateau was formed, John Boyd explained, of volcanic ash that had accumulated over a long period of time, not in one explosion, but many. Part of the stuff that fell was like fine sand, small particles of incandescent rock mixed with great quantities of steam. It billowed from the westward mountains in the form of a burning cloud. When the fury of explosion spent itself, what fell was mud, soft as a porridge that lay almost as level as a lake upon the surface of the existing landscape. Cooling, it hardened,

layer upon layer, like an enormous mudpie left to bake in the sun. Over the centuries rivulets of water draining snow and rain from the mountains carved wider channels. Wind and rain pockmarked the canyon walls. Birds and animals found shelter in the cavities. On the trail of the animals came man, whose hands shaped the yielding rock according to his need.

Edith Warner must have felt herself growing almost numb with new impressions. Out of masses of juniper and piñon the road emerged at last into a forest of tall western pine. The ground was matted with aromatic needles. Grama grass shone feathery in the afternoon sunlight. At the edge of a canyon the road abruptly ended. From here, John Boyd told her, all supplies for the ranch must be sent down by pack horse or slid in a basket on a long wire pulley. The guests had to walk more than a quarter of a mile down a dusty trail into the canyon. Worn out as she was, Edith Warner wondered if she would ever climb back up, if she would ever return to the familiar world she had left behind.

A sudden turn in the trail disclosed a crescent-shaped canyon, and far below, a narrow stream lined with alders as bright as the sunlight. On the other side of the Rito de los Frijoles—the little river of the beans—she saw the stone ranch house and guest cabins where her new life was to begin. That night she slept in the greatest quietness she had ever known.

For a long while she had strength to do little but rest. Then each day she found herself walking a little farther, climbing the mesa trails a little higher. At the top she would find a place where she could sleep for hours in the shelter of a sun-warmed rock. She waked feeling as though the strength of earth and sky had filled her. In later years this was to be one of her chief sources of renewal.

Edith tells in the beginning of her manuscript how surprised she was to learn that Frijoles Canyon had once been the home of a prehistoric people. The great ruin near the bottom of the old trail was called Tyúonyi. The School of American Research had conducted excavations there in 1908-09, and its walls now lay open and roofless like a fragment of honeycomb.

On the south-facing side of the canyon a steep talus led up to a sheer cliff. At the base of the cliff and high in the cliff wall were the

symmetrical openings of hollowed caves. The ceilings were still blackened with the smoke of long-ago fires. Etched into them were drawings—lively as children's—of animals, birds, masked beings, dancing men, symbols of rain and sun.

High in the wall of a cliff a mile above Tyúonyi there was an arched ledge of rock with a kiva in its floor, a hidden place of ceremony where men of old time rehearsed the mystery of their emergence into life and invoked the guardian spirits of their clan. The stream rippled beneath it through thickets of alder and willow. Trout flickered in the water. At twilight deer came down among the pines to drink.

It was hard to believe that five hundred years had passed since the people of Tyúonyi had laid down their tools and gone their unknown way. Their presence seemed as real to Edith as the sunlight on her skin. A woman might have been grinding only yesterday at this hollowed metate. A stone axe seemed warm from the grip of a man's hand. Wherever she walked fragments of boldly decorated pottery spoke of the ancient people's love of beauty. The earth seemed alive with the human essence of those who had danced their prayers upon it.

From John Boyd she learned to know the names of the cities that lay in grassy mounds of stone on the high mesas: Tsirege, Sankewi'i, Navawi'i, to the north Puyé and Shupinna. At Navawi'i where the mesa narrows, he showed her a deep pit hollowed in the rock where deer were once driven to their death by ancient hunters. Here she learned that Indians do not kill for pride or triumph as white men do, nor even heedlessly for their own need of food. They believe that man and deer both serve the purposes of life, that the deer will willingly let itself be slain if invoked with proper ceremony, if the will of the hunters is good, if their hearts are right.

On a perpendicular wall of rock at Tsirege she saw the Plumed Serpent marking the place where the trail goes up from the canyon bottom—a form of divinity associated by Indians with lakes and springs, with rain and running water. From the mounds of Sankewi'i, John Boyd pointed out in each direction a sacred mountain. On the tops of these mountains and in many high places of the plateau were shrines where the prayers of men were still planted

in the shape of little feathered wands, feathers to carry the needs of the people aloft to the powers which control the movements of clouds and of animals.

During these months in the canyon, Edith Warner came to feel that there are certain places in the earth where the great powers that move between earth and sky are much closer and more available than others, and that this region, this arid stretch of valley, plateau and circling mountain, was one of them. Was it the nature of the land itself, she wondered, some quality of rock, some effect of light or cloud or shaped horizon? Or was it because here the old and natural relationship and interdependence between man and the earth has for so long been kept fresh and new by the Indians?

The Pueblos have always believed that the earth they live upon is sacred. Each stone and bush and tree is alive with a spirit like their own. The gods lean from the clouds. They walk the earth in the shape of rain and of rainbows. When a man dies his spirit joins those of the Ancestors and comes with the clouds to rain upon the earth and make it fertile. It is the duty of all living men to maintain the harmony they are aware of in the world around them. They live in community not only with one another but with earth and sky, with plants and animals. They believe that the orderly functioning of the universe depends on them.

"Those first four months at Frijoles brought me the first conscious awareness of many things," said Edith. It was as though her groping spirit were putting forth roots, small tendrils of receptivity to the great forces of earth and sky that surged around her. She began to feel everywhere the persistence of a spirit that is more than mortal.

Some years later we found this entry in her journal.

My friend was wrong who said that this country was so old it does not matter what we Anglos do here. What we do anywhere matters but especially here. It matters very much. Mesas and mountains, rivers and trees, winds and rains are as sensitive to the actions and thought of humans as we are to their forces. They take into themselves what we give off and give it out again.

What the former inhabitants of the plateau had given off was now part of the essence of this land. She was beginning to learn what it means to live at the center of a sacred world.

THREE

ONE CRISP afternoon in late December, John Boyd asked Edith Warner to go with him on a trip to San Ildefonso, where he wanted to make arrangements for his guests to stay at the time of the pueblo's winter feast. They drove down from the plateau in the old topless Ford, its back seat loaded with Christmas candy for the children. They crossed the river over the old bridge at Buckman— the rickety structure I remember from childhood, which has long since been demolished. The road turned north from Buckman and wound upward along the east side of the lava-crowned mesa that the Indians call Shumo. At the top of a little rise the hill sloped downward into a world of brilliant light and shadow.

San Ildefonso lies in the Rio Grande Valley at the broad mouth of the Rio Nambé whose water, born in the Sangre de Cristo Range some twenty miles east, now scarcely ever reaches the great river. Irrigation ditches lead most of it off for alfalfa fields and orchards all up and down the valley. What little is left buries itself in the sand and feeds the roots of cottonwood trees that in autumn shine like a river of living gold. The rounded hills that guard the pueblo to the east are dotted with ovals of piñon and juniper. Beyond them the flesh-colored sediments have been sharply eroded into abstract planes and angles. The vegetation is sparse and inconspicuous. Only the sky above the mountains blossoms, in summer with white clouds that unfurl in gigantic flower forms, in winter with aurora-colored tides of sunset.

The Black Mesa stands square and solid at the margin of the river. A plum-colored ooze of hardened lava, it has been stripped of the sediments which once encased it and bears upon its flat summit a remnant of the former valley floor—marking the depth in time

through which the Rio Grande has carved its present channel. Indian mothers still discipline their children with tales of a giant who lives there in a deep cave and who will fetch them away to it if they are naughty.

The village has moved many times in its remembered past. It has been at its present location since the sixteenth century. The Spaniards, coming up from Mexico with their dream of golden cities, found mud-colored houses clustered around bare plazas just as they do today. In the south plaza the round kiva stands massive and silent except on feast days. Its ladder slants upward toward the sky; wide adobe steps lead outward and down to the ground smoothed by centuries of dancing feet. In the north plaza a cottonwood tree has widened its shadow through innumerable seasons.

In December the tree was leafless. Under the shelter of its greywhite branches children were playing who, as soon as they saw the tall "Anglo" ran to greet him like a favorite friend. They did not seem surprised to find his pockets full of candy, and soon all the round brown faces were bulging like chipmunks. They giggled and talked among themselves in whispers, small boys with enormous black eyes under their close-cropped hair, small girls with straight bangs hoisting children almost as big as themselves in competent brown arms.

The children stared at Edith like a flock of fledgling robins, not quite sure whether to be bold or shy. Merriment spilled out of their dark eyes, and she imagined how Frijoles Canyon once echoed with the laughter of children like these. How alike young things are in every time and place, she thought. And what a happy place to play this seemed—the hard-swept plaza, the rows of low houses fronting on it, some of the crooked door frames painted blue, some white, some natural weathered wood, the round shapes of adobe ovens like the kennels of friendly animals, the wagons and farming tools in the shelter of the great bare tree.

When the last bit of candy was devoured and the children had run off to their games or to relate the afternoon's adventure to their mothers, John Boyd took Edith with him to the house of his friend, Ignacio Aguilar. There was nothing special about Ignacio to mark that he was the religious leader of the pueblo. He was a little man

with eyes that seemed to her both shrewd and kind. His iron-grey
hair was drawn up and tied in a knot at his neck; bangs and long
side-locks framed his wrinkled face. He was dressed as a farming
man anywhere might be, in jeans and a sun-faded cotton shirt. The
dignity with which he greeted his visitors was that of a man to whom
courtesy comes as naturally as breathing.

"My house is yours," he said as he welcomed them in out of the
chill of the winter afternoon. The room into which they stepped
seemed spacious and uncluttered. The walls were white and
smooth; the ceiling was upheld by long pine beams. There was
little furniture. A few straight chairs and a couple of homemade
stools stood near the corner fireplace. A long blanket-roll against
one wall served as a seat by day and spread out to make a bed at
night. On a pole suspended from the vigas were arranged the family's ceremonial garments—striped blankets and buckskin leggings.
Holy pictures and a rosary hung on the wall. A couple of upright
sticks of piñon gave an astonishing amount of heat and a sweet
fragrance like the essence of summer days.

Edith sat quietly by the fireplace while the two men talked together. On the way down from the plateau John Boyd had told her
a little about Ignacio. She knew the gnarled hands that rested on
his knees had scattered wheat for many plantings and heaped the
corn for many huskings, that they could tan a deerskin so that it was
soft and white for moccasins. All the trails as well as the plants of
mountain and mesa were known to him. He had been trained in
the ritual of the Mass and served the Mission priest throughout
his life. In addition there had been handed down to him by word
of mouth the vast and ancient knowledge essential for the position
he held in the pueblo. It was his responsibility to watch over the
pattern of daily life in his village, the detail of ceremonial observ-
ance whereby man is made conscious of the part he plays among
the seasons and the elements. Above everything he must keep himself free from disturbing thoughts. He must pray and fast often.
Over and over he must remind his people that the good of the village
depends upon the strength and energy with which each man in his
heart wills what is good.

Susana, Ignacio's wife, could speak no word of English but she

managed to express her friendliness in other ways. Ignacio's son, Joe, had married a girl from Picuris, one of the northern pueblos. Rosalie had learned to speak Tewa, the language of San Ildefonso, and fitted into the family and village life as though she had been born there. Her mother-in-law had taught her to make the pottery for which the San Ildefonso women are famous. On a ledge near the fireplace stood a row of polished bowls, and, with her shy smile, Susana placed one in Edith's hands. Around its margin, etched in dull black on glossy black, she marveled to see the outline of the Plumed Serpent—the same figure John Boyd had shown her drawn on the rock at Tsirege. The design was conventionalized, almost as abstract as a Greek border except for the head with its backward-pointing plume and the zigzag lightning issuing from its mouth. A motif of terraced cloud was repeated in each undulation of the body. Edith found herself thinking of the winding thrust of the river, of the stab of lightning in the dark folded clouds, of dry earth pounded by long lines of rain. The Plumed Serpent, she began to realize, was no literal reptile, but one of the most ancient metaphors of human thought. Not the river, but the force embodied in the river; not the cloud but the life-giving energies within the cloud— these are what the image of the Plumed Serpent speaks of to the Pueblo people and to all who know that rain is one of the many forms of deity.

From the first, Edith knew enough never to question an Indian about his mysteries. What she learned through the years she learned as silently as she did from stones or trees, from rivers and mesas, as she now did from the feel under her fingers of this bowl that a woman's brown hands had finished in beauty, out of a wisdom older than any word.

It was several months later that Ignacio told her the story of the Plumed Serpent, Awanyu. She had grown by then to love the San Ildefonso people, and the Aguilar family made her welcome when-ever she came there. One summer day she had ridden horseback to the pueblo. It had been a long journey from the mountains, across the sun-drenched mesas, down the narrow trail among the fallen black boulders, and across the river. In the cool of the evening Ignacio placed chairs outside the doorway. Relaxing after the long

day's ride, she rested her head against the adobe wall of the house. She watched the afterglow touch the kiva, the curved mesas across the river, the long mesa to the south, Shumo. The evening star shone out above the rim of the western mesa. Under the great cottonwood tree in the north plaza the pueblo boys were singing an age-old song. Edith felt at home, as if she had come again to some familiar moment of childhood—a childhood that belongs to us all, though farther away and longer ago than our memories.

It was a moment that was ripe for stories, the old tales men sometimes tell their children in the half-light. Ignacio had been smoking a cigarette, not nervously, she noticed, as most white people do, but slowly, tranquilly, as though the inhaling of each breath were a sacred gesture. When the last blue feather of smoke had vanished he began to speak in a voice that was as brittle as the rustle of dry leaves.

"Now I tell you about Awanyu," he began. His face was almost invisible in the darkness, yet she could feel his eyes on hers intent as a watchful bird. His words were simple as though he were speaking to a child.

"He lives many miles away in a deep lake. Sometimes he does not come for many months. We plant corn and wheat but the ground is hard. They come up. They grow a little, but if no rain comes, they die. We have no *atole*, no bread for winter." His old voice trembled as though he were remembering centuries of hunger. "Then we pray and dance," he went on strongly, "all the men and women and children. We dance all day and all night. And when we dance, if our hearts are right, he comes. No matter if the ice be *that* thick"—and Ignacio held his hand several feet above the ground, "he breaks through and comes in the black cloud!"

Edith felt he did not merely believe this story as legend. It was something he knew as surely as men know that each day the sun rises.

"If, when we dance, our hearts are right, the rain will come."

"If our hearts are right . . ." These words stirred something deep in Edith Warner. She began to realize that the Pueblo dances are not simply magical devices to control the forces of nature. They are a means by which men bring their own lives into harmony with the order and beauty of the world around them.

"In the beautiful still world," Edith says in her narrative, "I kept pondering Ignacio's words." She was still pondering them on that August day nearly twenty-five years later when the report of the atomic bomb flashed round the world from devastated Hiroshima, the bomb that had been made at Los Alamos, only twenty-five miles from San Ildefonso where the Indians still dance in summer to help the green corn grow.

"I am not, and never have been, the guiding hand in my life," Edith writes in the first of her Christmas letters. "Something—what, I do not venture to say—has prevented what I thought I wanted to do and pushed me into what I eventually did."

In the spring of her first year in New Mexico the Boyds gave up the guest ranch in Frijoles and moved to an unsettled valley high in the Jemez Mountains. Restless adventurer that he was, John Boyd could never contentedly stay long in one place. His wife thought wistfully of the comfortable farm life in Indiana where they had lived in the first years of their marriage. She was a friendly woman who found the greatest delight in church socials and busy neighboring, but she adored her husband and followed him from one lonely place in New Mexico to another throughout his life. It was Martha Boyd who taught Edith Warner what women who must cope with daily living on the edge of a wilderness need to know. During her four months at Frijoles the Boyds became to her like second parents, and when they left the canyon they took her with them.

The last lap of the two-day journey was made in a wagon. For a while they slept in tents at the edge of a little clearing surrounded by fir and aspen. Then they built a log cabin with a corral beside it. Water had to be carried in buckets across a narrow footbridge from a spring on the opposite side of the ice-cold stream. The women wrestled with an old cookstove and an uncertain supply of wood that burned stubbornly. Long-range planning and ingenuity were required to feed the hungry men who worked all day cutting and hauling logs for the new buildings and laying them in place. Food was shipped from Santa Fe to the old siding at Buckman by freight,

and hauled from there by wagon up the long hill, along the mesa, then over the mountainside into the Valle Grande where only faint wagon tracks showed through the grass. Fresh vegetables and fruit were rare luxuries. A high point of that summer was a basket of apricots brought in by wagon from Jemez Springs many rough miles to the south. The mail came once a week. It was often Edith who rode horseback for it, over the lonely trail past Vallecitos de los Indios, down the steep red-rocked canyon, past the old ruin of a Spanish mission to the little village of Jemez Springs—and back again. The trip took nearly a whole day.

Edith told me how she used to think, during these long rides, of the dreary mornings when she stood shivering on a street corner in Philadelphia, waiting for a bus to take her to the school where she was teaching, wondering how she could live through another day of it. This spring in the Valle she watched the first shimmer of green on the white aspens. Each day the color spread and became a little denser but never matched the darkness of the evergreens. White violets began to bloom along the stream. Later there were wild strawberries along the sunny slopes. In the Valle Grande, lambs on wobbly legs filled the air with their bleating. The winds had blown bitterly at first, but Martha Boyd comforted Edith on days when her nerves began to fray, saying, "The wind will go down with the sun."

The life was hard, and she found herself longing for the desert landscape with its magic lights and colors, the Rio Grande gleaming like a great bronze snake in the waste of black rocks tumbled from the mesa. She knew that her year of freedom in New Mexico was almost over, and yet, if she could, she must find a way to stay.

Edith's family, who loved her and never ceased to admire her spirit and her courage, were willing to help her to the limit of their ability—yet she never got over the feeling that it was she who should have been helping them. When she left the Boyds in the fall of 1923 her sister Vel, now Mrs. Benjamin Ludlow, came out to Albuquerque and got a job so that Edith would not have to return East for another year. This was the beginning of a very close relationship between the sisters, and until she married, Vel returned to visit Edith at Otowi almost every summer.

Nothing but sheer determination kept Edith going through the four years that followed. After the tutoring job with the Smithwicks she returned East for a few years but suffered from such ill health that she was forced to go back to the Southwest. For a time she was a patient at the Tilden Health School in Denver, and later on its staff. In 1928 she returned to New Mexico and the discouraging task of hunting an occupation. Her ideas of how to make a living in that sparsely settled country were numerous, she says, but impractical for an unmarried woman of thirty-five with no financial resources. The most impractical of these ideas did not compare with the job that Fate, half-smiling, half-severe, seems to have had in mind for Edith Warner from the very beginning.

FIVE

THREE miles from San Ildefonso Pueblo across the bridge on the road to Los Alamos was a shabby little house that Edith Warner had always thought looked particularly out-of-place in New Mexico where for centuries flat-roofed adobe houses had been built to blend with the earth from which their sunbaked bricks were made. The land it stood on belonged to an Indian family at the pueblo, but none of them would have dreamed of living there. They might have tried to grow a field of corn or beans, but the ground was too high above the river for irrigation. Long ago one of the Indians had planted a small orchard near the edge of the sandy arroyo that enters the river from the west. He would walk over each day in summer to tend it, but at night he always returned to the comfortable companionship of his wife and small children who greeted him with cries of "Tay-tay"—Grandfather—as they ran out to take his hand and lead him into supper.

The little house stood beside a dingy boxcar railway station not far from the tracks of the Denver & Rio Grande narrow-gauge railroad that until late in 1941 ran between Santa Fe and Antonito, Colorado. In the early twenties a one-lane suspension bridge was built beside the old railway trestle, the old crossing at Buckman was abandoned, and Otowi became the unloading point for all mail and supplies that were shipped to Los Alamos School from Santa Fe. A truck was sent down to take them the rest of the way, but it made the trip up the steep switchback road only three times weekly. In between times, someone living at the station had to see to unloading the freight and keep watch against possible marauders.

At first the caretaker had been a Portuguese Basque named Shorty, who used to work at a logging camp situated on the south

side of the road. Two rooms of the little house had been part of the camp, and when logging operations ceased Shorty acquired the house for his own use. He rented an acre of land from a San Ildefonso family and then proceeded to move the house across the tracks. After adding a room and digging a well, Shorty opened a store which offered the few passersby soft drinks, tobacco and canned food. During Prohibition he augmented his tiny income by selling bootleg whiskey. One day the law must have come sniffing a bit too close on Shorty's trail for comfort, for he suddenly vanished, leaving no one now who even remembers his proper name.

When Shorty left, Adam, a young San Ildefonso Indian, consented for a while to act as watchman. His father and mother, Julián and María Martínez—the famous potters—bought the house, since it stood on their land; and Adam, after adding a fourth room, took his wife to live there. They found it lonely, in spite of the two toylike trains that ran by each day, and soon returned to the deeply rooted communal life of their pueblo. This left the little house unoccupied, the freight unguarded.

On the day that Edith Warner had exhausted the last known possibility for earning a living in Santa Fe, she met Mr. Connell, the director of Los Alamos School, at a hotel in Santa Fe. At his wits' end, looking for someone—by that time anyone—to stay at Otowi, he offered her the job.

He knew almost nothing about her. He only knew that she wanted desperately to remain in the country. He was a man of determined character who usually managed to obtain any objective he set his mind to, and he had a strong Irish streak which persuaded him to deal with people on the basis of his hunches.

He did his best, in his smooth Irish way, to make the job sound glamorous. "You can rent the house for very little," he told her. "María and Julián own it. Their son, Adam, will come over to unload the freight for you. All you have to do is see that he gets there on time. We will pay you twenty-five dollars a month." He sounded as though he thought it was a princely sum. At least it would be better than nothing, she told herself. With her long experience in frugal living she might make it do.

"That will cover the rent and Adam's wages," Mr. Connell con-

tinued. Edith's heart sank. How did he expect her to live, she wondered? Did he think the birds would feed her? "Of course the profits of the store will all be yours," he had added quickly. "And with you living there, no one will attempt theft."

Surely desperation had addled his wits a little, she thought. Frail and reticent as she had always been, how could anyone possibly take her for a watchdog? At the bridge she would be entirely alone except for the few passersby, Indians, sheepherders, an occasional tourist, no other human being within shouting distance, not even a telephone except the railway instrument which was unavailable for private use. Her only link with the world would be the truck from the school, and the trains that often whistled past without stopping. Her nearest neighbors would be the Indians at the pueblo, a long walk on the other side of the river.

The whole plan seemed completely fantastic. Surely there could be no one as little suited for such a job. Yet to wait for another opportunity would be too great a gamble. The meager resources with which her family had been helping through her illness had been exhausted. A decision had to be made at once. Return East she would not, of that much she was certain. This offer would tide her over for a little, would give her time to look for a better solution.

"How soon can you take over?" the determined voice was asking.

"I can start any time," she heard herself say, amazed, as though she listened to some stranger.

SIX

Spring was late again in 1928. On the first day of May at Otowi not one shiny green leaf brightened the gray branches of the cottonwoods in the bend of the river. The wind had been blowing for days and the sky was leaden with dust. Sand whirled along the margins of the river.

When she stepped across the splintered threshold of the little house, Edith wondered what madness had possessed her. The boards in the floor were cracked. Knotholes had been patched with pieces of tin. The ceilings were made of sagging and faded wallboard. In one room there was no ceiling at all, only the weather-stained boards that formed the low-peaked roof. The dingy windows let in hardly enough light to see by. There were no cupboards or closets of any kind. It seemed impossible to hope that the untidy little shack could ever be made into a place of peace and beauty.

It had been one of Edith's wild dreams, in the weeks since Mr. Connell had persuaded her to live there, that in addition to selling gasoline and cokes she might run the place as a tearoom. She could serve fresh bread and homemade cookies to the groups of boys who occasionally came down from the school to swim in a protected arm of the river. She had a special recipe for chocolate cake. Santa Fe was already a tourist center and visitors on their way to Frijoles were crossing the bridge at Otowi in increasing numbers. She might be able to fix up a room for occasional paying guests, women like herself who needed a few weeks of solitude to restore bodies and spirits frayed by the confusion of city living. Today Edith only found herself wondering how long she could manage to survive.

Fortunately there was work to be done. In the room that had been

the store her few belongings waited to be unpacked. These consisted of a couple of trunks, some boxes of books, a barrel of dishes, two folding beds and four straight chairs. Her mother, she knew, would have told her there was no time to be wasted in discouragement. She found herself thinking of her little German grandmother who as a bereaved and timid young girl had packed her thick Lutheran books in a wooden chest and set sail for a new life in America. It seemed as though the spirits of all women, who since humanity's beginning have made homes in wilderness, came now to companion her like an invisible chorus. Perhaps the trouble with the little house, she thought, was that only rootless men had used it for a shelter. No woman had ever tried to fill it with human warmth and make it beautiful. At least she must try to overcome her own feeling of dismay and establish some pattern for temporary living.

Woman-like, she started at once on the middle room which was to be the kitchen. By evening she had succeeded in making that one room habitable. A Navajo rug on the floor worked a magic of symmetry and color. Empty packing boxes became a table and cupboard. A soft-colored Chimayo blanket turned one of the narrow beds into a couch. A ticking clock, a pot of ivy on a high sill, a teakettle singing on the range—it was as though the heart of the little house had begun to beat.

Edith kept herself so busy all day that she was hardly conscious of the world outside the house. The afternoon train whistled shrilly for the crossing and rattled south without stopping. Now and then she heard a car pass over the bridge. The wind that had battered against the walls all day died at evening, and everything became still. After supper she went to sit on the steps outside the kitchen door. The only sound was made by the rushing Rio Grande, swollen by melting snow.

The Rio Grande at Otowi is a tawny color, heavy with sand and silt swept down from the high mountains of Colorado and northern New Mexico. Clear and clean in its origin, it ripples, cascades, twines among the roots of grasses and old trees, pulling out little by little the stitches and seams of earth, dissolving, loosening, trans-

porting mountain slopes grain by grain onto the level land. Flowing out from the base of the mountains, it splits the black, basaltic crust that shields the plain. It wedges itself down through the high-piled gravels of vanished times and climates. Arroyos, sandy drainage-gutters for the violent summer rains, empty their fierce burdens of rolling earth and rock into the river. The Chama enters from the west, stained with the red sandstones beyond Gallina, with the yellow clay of Tierra Amarilla. After the Chama enters the water is never clear again until it is lost in the Gulf of Mexico, swept away and dispersed in the blind tides of ocean.

Just below the bridge at Otowi the river which has been spreading widely between its gravelly banks begins to flow past strong resistant rock into a canyon formed by two great mesas. The Indians call the spot Po-sah-con-gay, "the place where the river makes a noise." As she listened that night, Edith Warner began to hear more than meaningless noise in the sound of the water. The river seemed to make of its noise a song, a song she told me she thought of through the years as the melody of living. She watched the darkness well up out of the valley like a tide rising from the bottom of an extinct sea. For awhile, after the sun went down, the sky at the edge of the eastern horizon grew more luminous. The mountains flushed with rose that faded slowly. The two mesas on each side of the river seemed to grow larger as though they were being drawn from the earth by a giant hand. The one on the east the Indians called Shumo, on the west To-tavi. The band of dark lava crowning them made them look awesome to Edith but not fearful. "They are like two ancient beings who have seen much," she thought. For many thousands of years the river had torn its way between these mesas. Clouds had burst over them, dusty winds assailed them. The sky had leaned upon them with all its weight of light and darkness. Now they stood firm, balanced between the upthrusting, the down-pulling forces in the earth. In these strong shapes time itself became visible, time that works through the years to bring forth from all things the lines of essential beauty hidden in them.

As the stars began one by one to fill the deep sky above her, Edith Warner found the great age and deep-rootedness of the mesas com-

forting. Through them she felt connected with a source of strength within herself, something as old as the mesas, as wise, as unshakable. Utterly alone though she was on this first evening, she felt that the wordless land had accepted her and that if she too had endurance, life in the little house could be deeply satisfying.

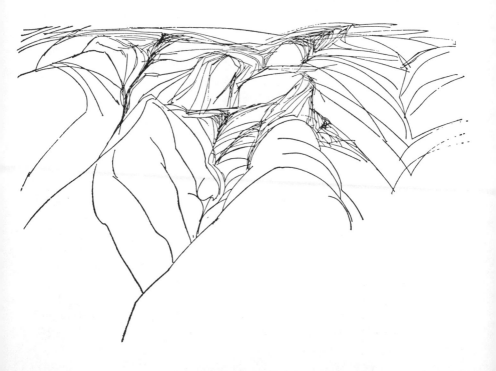

SEVEN

THE SECOND DAY was cold and rainy. Toward afternoon Edith heard hoofbeats on the bridge and looked out to see two young Indians entering the yard on horseback. One of them was Adam. Though she had seen him only twice before, on this lonely morning he seemed like an old friend. When they had dismounted he greeted her with a shy smile and said, "This is my cousin Richard. I brought him to help me unload the oats. The trainmen want to take the empty car tomorrow."

As they discussed the weather and the freight arrangements she saw that these cousins were alike only in their sense of humor and the way in which they wore their hair. Even in those days many of the younger Indians continued to keep their hair cut short after they finished school. But Adam and Richard let theirs grow, parted it in the middle, tied it with yarn and brought the braids forward to hang over their shoulders. Adam was short and compactly built, while Richard was lean and loose-limbed, with what Edith has described as the eyes of a mystic.

When the oats had been taken care of, she asked the two young men to come into the house to get warm. They were her first guests, and she eagerly made them tea. Wet and cold as they were, they drank it as though it were their favorite beverage. Later Edith learned always to keep a pot of coffee boiling for her Indian neighbors who could drink it all day long. Luckily she had already made a batch of oatmeal cookies, and she watched them disappear while her visitors looked bashfully about. At first all three were at loss for conversation. Finally Richard said solemnly of the packing box around which they had been sitting, "This is a good table you made." Laughter broke the restraint and then Adam said, "Already

the house is different. It looks nice." As they left he turned to her and asked with a real note of concern, "You aren't afraid here by yourself?"

"Not very much," she assured him, yet that night as mist and darkness shut out her guarding mesas she found herself facing for the first time "this thing called being afraid." The solitude itself did not alarm her. "I feel very small and of little worth in the presence of great spaces and deep silence," she said, "but not afraid." Having so little of material worth and a locked door she told herself, she had no reason to fear man. Only those who have security must be concerned lest they lose it. But in spite of her brave thoughts, she felt a vague uneasiness.

Just what she would have done in case robbery of the station were attempted she never knew. A few weeks later someone gave her a revolver and the grapevine carried word through the valley that loiterers after dark would be asked no questions. One night she awoke with an uneasy feeling that someone was near. Clouds partially covered the moon, but there was enough light for her to see a man run from the screen door toward the bridge where he had tied his horse. She opened the door and clutched the gun with trembling hands. As she fired a shot into the air, horse and rider galloped away, and she was again alone in the stillness of the night.

At the end of the first week a woman friend came out from the East to stay through the summer and help get the house in shape. A practical nurse by profession, Lottie Weidaw was older and more experienced than Edith; she was ruggedly built and possessed of a good sense of humor which offset her tendency to be somewhat dour. Independent though the women hoped to be, it soon became evident that the work was more than the two of them could accomplish. A man was needed to build cupboards and closets, to cut windows in the corner room, to make a fireplace. Without an automobile, with scarcely any money to pay wages, how could they find anyone to work for them?

Then Edith thought of Ignacio, her old friend at the pueblo whose story of Awanyu had first set her heart upon this path of life. Perhaps he would know someone at the pueblo who could help them.

As the women crossed the bridge and walked the long road to the village, Edith remembered the first time she had gone to San Ildefonso with John Boyd. On that day it had been a land golden under the afternoon sun, with clouds casting their shadows as they moved like great birds in a blue sky. Today the cottonwoods along the river had green leaves and in the fields beside the road spring wheat was pushing up through the bare earth. Chamisa was changing its winter gray for a soft new green. After they passed the wide arroyo the road wound between low hills and fields where fragrant wild plum thickets bloomed along the acequias. There was smoke rising from the chimneys of the pueblo, and beyond it the Black Mesa standing alone beside the river. The Indians call the mesa Tunyo, which means "a spot by itself."

As they drew near Ignacio's house, Florencita, the granddaughter whom Edith had first known as a toddler ran to meet them. She had grown to look like her mother, Rosalie, with big eyes as black as the bangs above them and a broad smile. Her English was limited to "hello," "goodbye," "candy," and "thank you," but this was never an obstacle to the games she kept urging Edith to play with her. Soon Rosalie came to the door and with a smile said, "Oh, you come at last. We've been looking for you. Come in."

When she asked for Ignacio, Rosalie consulted her mother-in-law, Susana. Then she said, "My father and Joe are in the fields down near the river, but they will come soon. My mother says you must wait."

While Lottie busied herself exploring, Edith went to sit on the doorstep with the children. In this country, she had discovered, there is need to sit quietly now and then—to look, to listen, to feel. Even the children were quiet as they ate tortillas. The shadow of the round kiva lengthened across the swept earth of the plaza as it had on that other summer evening. It was hard to realize that six years had passed. Now she had come to live as neighbor to the people of San Ildefonso, and to share their sacred world.

A sound of wagon wheels woke her at last from her reverie. The children shouted "Tay-tay" as they ran to meet their grandfather. Soon they came round the corner of the house clinging to Ignacio's hands, telling him how long his visitors had been waiting. After

greetings and the casual words that always prepare the way for real Pueblo conversation, Edith explained her need. Ignacio and the women talked together at great length in Tewa. Then he told her he thought his son Joe might help them. "He can take you to town in his car for the things you need. Then he will go there to do his work. When he comes in we'll ask him and see what he says."

Ignacio's idea was just what she had hoped for and she eagerly waited for Joe to finish putting up the horses. When he came in he greeted the visitors with friendliness and humor. "Why don't you catch some of the burros down there so you won't have to walk?" he asked. After a good laugh the way opened easily for them to work together. Joe agreed to his father's proposal, he was willing to let her pay as she was able, and the two women walked back to the river and over the bridge again with the warm glow of knowing they were no longer strangers in the valley.

Having Lottie with her that summer was a great blessing for Edith. She knew she could never have survived the difficult first months without the older woman's help. However, it was not long before she realized that her need for solitude was greater than her need for companionship and that as soon as she could she must go her way alone. After Lottie moved to Santa Fe where she could more easily practice as a nurse, Edith usually had friends with her only for short visits. Her life was filled by the guests she served in increasing numbers and by her warm contacts with the Indians at the pueblo.

It was through the problem of remodeling the little house that Edith's life first began to be knit with the San Ildefonso people.

From the beginning they felt a pride in being able to help her. Realizing how close she lived, like themselves, to the verge of poverty, there was none of the sense of patronage so many Indians feel with white people who are endlessly trying to "improve" things for them. Joe Aguilar turned out not only handsome but dependable and the work went swiftly—swiftly at least for this land where time is not marked off into hurrying segments but ripens according to ancient rhythms like the fruit of a tree.

Before the tearoom was entirely ready for business, people began stopping in to ask for cold drinks and sandwiches. Ice came out from Santa Fe on the freight train. Between freight days Coca-Cola bottles were hung in the well. Butter and milk were kept in a "desert refrigerator" cooled by evaporation.

At first the only customers were those who were native to the region, their pockets often as penniless as Edith's. Spanish-Americans galloped up to the door and asked for "tobaccy Dukey," for crackers and sardines. Covered wagons crossed the bridge and stopped beside the road. From under their canvas covers little children looked out, while an older boy and girl might climb down over the wheel and run in to ask "Have you a store? How many candies for a nickel?" Sometimes they wanted cigarettes for the father who held the horses, or a lemon for a coughing child. The whole family would be on the way to their ranchito up on the plateau where they planted pinto beans. All summer long the wagons went up and down from the bean fields above to the chile fields below. Edith found she missed them when the harvest was over and the children went back to school.

All sorts of cars from Model T's to occasional Packards stopped for gasoline at the old pump. The hand crank was so hard to work that she was relieved when the driver wanted only two gallons, even though such a small quantity did not pay. If the driver told her to fill the tank she learned to suspect that he might say "I pay you pretty soon, maybe next time I sell a calf." Sometimes the calf was never sold and her meager profit for the month would be wiped out.

One day when she was especially discouraged an old man and his son came in for sandwiches and coffee. They were both incredibly homely, with the heavy odor about them of clothes and bodies

long unwashed. They had come down to the valley from their little bean ranch near Los Alamos to celebrate the feast of Santiago. Now they were waiting to go home in the mail truck. It was almost noon and the walk across the valley had made them thirsty. When Edith filled their cups a second time the old man asked how much he owed. She knew his family was large and his ranch small, so the amount she asked was half the usual charge. When he paid he shook her hand and said, "I always like to help a poor lone woman." She thought his "help" referred to the lunch he had bought. It was only after he left that she found the dime he had left under his plate.

"I decided then that there are compensations for being 'poor' and 'lone,' " she tells us.

So slim her margin always was that most of the time there was no margin at all, when even a dime under the plate could tip the precarious balance. There were times when the whole venture would seem impossible, when she felt as though she were clinging by her fingertips to the brittle edge of a precipice. If she let go it would mean destruction, not just of the business that was her livelihood but of the web of peace and beauty her spirit had begun so delicately to spin out of itself. Yet no matter how marginless her existence, how uncertain the immediate future, she learned that in time a solution would present itself.

During the fifth year of her life in the little house, she made this entry in her journal:

This afternoon as I ironed, I was thinking about money. Unexpectedly during the week enough had come in to pay a bill that I did not see how I could meet. I recalled how frequently that had happened when I had done what seemed to me my utmost. I recalled, too, how a wise old man had taught me not to worry about such things. But habit is strong, nor have I learned to live as simply as he. Yet each year I do less of the customary things of our civilization.

EIGHT

IN THE BEGINNING the Indians at the pueblo found it hard to understand how Edith Warner could live alone at the-place-where-the-river-makes a-noise. How anyone could live alone was a mystery to them, much less a fragile little white woman in her early thirties with no sign of a husband or any other family. It was unheard of for an Indian's life not to be bound up in community. Even their prayers were communal, the great seasonal dances where long lines of men and women and often tiny children merged into one pattern of movement and sound and color.

The Indians have established a moving relationship with the land they dwell in. They live in community not only with each other but with earth and sky, with plants and animals. They consciously play their part in maintaining the wholeness of the universe; wholeness or holiness—it is more than a play on words. It is the recognition of the common spirit that animates all life.

I have never forgotten a dance I watched at Taos Pueblo one winter afternoon. Entering the pueblo lands was like crossing an invisible line into another world. The gray branches of the wild plum coiling like smoke along the borders of the unploughed fields, willows glowing warm beside the stream, the tall shape of leafless cottonwoods, the silent vegetation, the guardian mountain—it was as though industrial man and all his works had been forgotten or had not yet been dreamed.

The pueblo was clean and bare in the winter sun. On the rooftops a few women were gathered in their colored shawls, with small children leaning against them, waiting, expectant. Suddenly there came a hurrying chorus of men, fifteen, perhaps, or twenty. Two of them carried a huge gray dried hide folded lengthwise. Some of the others held small drums; the rest carried notched sticks. They

gathered in front of the arched gateway to the church and each pulled a low stool from behind the wall. Seated in an oval around the spread hide they began drumming and chanting softly.

From three directions came groups of young girls and men, each group singing by itself, with no concern for the confusion of sound as the groups came together. The girls formed a circle around the seated chorus, stretched out their arms, their spread fingers making a repetitive gesture as though they were gently smoothing the sown earth. Round in a circle they moved, smiling, delicately treading, their arms rayed toward the center where the dark mystery was being entreated, a mystery that was at the same time joyful and full of gaiety. Around the women moved a great circle of men, round and round to the right, walking, not dancing, closely formed. Beyond the two circles it was almost impossible to see the faces of the singing men at the center. The voices were gentle, yet full of power. The drums beat softly in a pattern of sound repeated over and over, the rhythm exact and undeviating in every measure.

At the end of the movement sudden cries, as though in triumph. Then a brief interval of silence, of relaxation; then the same pattern repeated endlessly, patiently, but each time, though the movement of the dance was exactly the same, the detail of the song was varied. The motions of the young girls were gentle and caressing as though they were radiating power from the tips of their fingers into whatever lay at the center of the circle. Continuing throughout the movement was a strange sound, the back-and-forth sawing of notched sticks. At the end of the afternoon the circle suddenly loosened; the grouped figures went off in their several directions toward the kivas, laughing, at ease, gay like children who have played together for an afternoon.

No wonder, I thought, that we white people watch the Indian ceremonials with such envy. We have not lived long enough on this continent to mingle its earth with our dreams. No wonder, too, that Edith Warner, in spite of her closeness to the Pueblo people—or even because of it—was often very lonely.

"I remember asking her almost casually once," her goddaughter, Peter Miller, wrote me, "if she wasn't sorry not to be an Indian, and realizing from her answer how awful it was to be shut out from

sharing by her white skin." It was not her white skin so much as all that lived inside it, that long inheritance of history and culture from far away lands which makes us seem alien still to our Indian neighbors.

"Since there was so little of the Indian ritual she was able to share," Peter's letter continues, "she made her own out of simple, natural things. Gathering pine knots was part of it—'those multi-shaped legacies of long-forgotten trees'—lighting the Christmas fire, the first spring seed-sowing, the first snow in fall, the spring and autumn flight of the wild geese—this most especially, and all these things linked to the rhythm of earth and her life upon it. She used often to go to 'high places.' . . . She said it was a thing found in all religions—the need to go *up* for meditation. . . . She had a little shrine on To-tavi that she went to often. To-tavi seemed like an arm to her, a great sheltering embrace. In the very middle of that embrace she made a tiny shrine, just off the trail and so inconspicuous that I've often walked past it even when I was looking for it. In those last days before she died she used to send me there to tend it almost every day. I suppose she did it more for me than for herself, knowing that it was impossible to feel there anything but joy.

"You know how much involved she was in the life of the village. The gradual loss of ritual was terribly tragic to bear, and it was in this connection that she found it hardest to wait, not to push forward on her own instincts, but wait to be guided. It was a real torment to her often not to be able to leap into a gap and say what she felt. And sometimes she did. The lesson had to be learned again—wait, wait for the time to be ripe, wait for somebody to be able to bear the words."

In her own journal Edith tells us:

One learns through the years to stand alone and to find within one's own soul most of what one needs. But there are times when the utter aloneness and apartness overshadows the compensations; when all the treasured little things such as Sayah's "my grandchild," Quebi's "I wish you were going too," Oqua's long-planned Christmas gift, turn to ashes. Nana would tell me at such a time to say a prayer and sing, forgetting myself.

And yet in spite of her inner loneliness Edith shared the human bond to an extent that is seldom possible for any white person. In one of her few published essays (*Neighborhood, A Settlement Quarterly*, June 1931) Edith describes the rainbowlike weaving of these strands of friendship:

"Their acceptance of me has been so gradual through these three years that I can scarcely mark its progress, and yet there are certain steps that stand out. True, I did not come as an entire stranger, for years ago I was taken to several homes in the Pueblo by a mutual friend and accepted for that reason. But to most of them I was scarcely known, a white woman come to live on their reservation two miles from the village. Now, when I am invited to come into the kitchen or the inner family room, I know I am counted as a friend. And if, when I chance to visit a home at meal time, an extra cup and plate are placed, and I am asked to share the meal, I know I am, as Quebi said, 'one of us.' Sometimes it has seemed slow progress where natural contacts are few, but when friendship is given, it is not a passing thing. Now I am greeted in Tewa, some times followed by 'you haven't been here for so long!'

"Always have I wanted a home that might be open house to my friends, and from the very beginning of this crude one, folks have come in at the kitchen door, opened to the sun and the song of the river. Uh-de and O-pah-mu-nu were the first in those days when I served tea on a packing-box table, and since that rainy afternoon many a friendly word has passed over a cup of *café* or tea. . . . Sunday is frequently 'at home' day and no unusual sight is a wagon or car crossing the bridge with gay-shawled women, bright-shirted men and black-eyed children come to visit. Sometimes there is a friendly silence, sometimes animated conversation, but always magazines and papers are scanned. Many weighty matters have been discussed under its rough board ceiling and much laughter has there been by sunlight and candlelight.

"Holidays and birthdays are reason enough for one family or another around the long table, with all the special things most folks enjoy. Sometimes it is just a fireside meal, with songs and tale-telling for dessert. . . . Sometimes the men move the furniture,

bring two hollow-log drums, and we dance to the beat of the *tombé* and the clearvoiced song of the drummers. Babies fall asleep to the familiar music and are laid on a bed. Children run in and out, or dance too, but are seldom in the way or misbehaved. And we grownups forget all else and dance together, young and old. Being accustomed now to unexpected guests, I am not perturbed but glad when along the road comes a familiar blanketed figure. There is always food, should our meal be finished, and somehow I am never too busy to prepare it for Ci-ya-pe. Sometimes there are two, one bent with a stout stick for a brown hand, a battered black hat on the thin graying hair, the 'Old One' from Nambe, come walking to see me and to eat in my house. That is an honor.

"Always in the Pueblo there is an extra cup of coffee in the pot for me, a tortilla or *bua* in the basket, and I find it a real pleasure to share those meals, especially if they are eaten in the Indian fashion. No matter how little or much, it is willingly shared. One day I could stay just a few minutes and Kun-povi may have felt reluctance in offering me their supper, but she handed me a cup of water, making me in that way share the meal. I wonder if she sensed how much that tin of cold water meant to me!

"The fireplace is the center of a home in this country and it is always there the chairs are drawn after a meal, and to it a guest is invited to come. At first I sat formally on a chair, but now I feel free to do as instinct bids me, and sit on a low stool or the hearth. I really like to, and then it tends to break down any barriers of difference that might seem to exist. Somehow they stand out in my living here, those fireside hours. One was in an inner room on an evening when the men were busy and we women talked about the babies and about ourselves, as women always have, and knew each other better. One was serious talk of the old order changing, with my hostess urging me to spend the night; on another, such fascinating tales I scarcely could leave. And one never-to-be-forgotten night, I walked to the village in the moonlight to sit on the floor beside the fire while the Old One sang songs for me until midnight. About six words I understood, but I needed no language to feel the charm of his thin, but still musical voice, and the twinkling eyes in his expressive face.

"Such kindly thoughtful things they have done. In the beginning when I was tenderfoot enough to think I could raise vegetables with no acequia for irrigation, it was he whom I call *Padre* who came to plough my garden. I was his daughter, he said, and he did it gladly for me. He has never been too busy or tired to hear my troubles and give advice or comfort. And didn't he go hunting an herb to make well my sick knee? It was 'Uncle John' who, seeing me gathering some sticks along the river bank, thought I needed wood and came bringing a load. It is his needle that mends my moccasins, with never a time of payment, and always he greets me with a cheery 'What can I do for you today?' . . . One other has come often to see how things went with me or if I needed something, and when Nana-tsideh's white horse comes trotting across the bridge, all the hard and the glad things kept for his understanding ear come to the surface. There is always some door or window to be fixed, a tree planted, a chair mended. And when I have to get away from all of civilization, it is two horses he brings to take me up on the mesas where clean winds blow and there is only silence and sunshine. Sometimes it is Oqua-pi's horse, and I know now that I can never pay in coin for my rides on Lady's back. And Po-sta's voice was sincere when it rang out above the children's prattle. 'How did you like my horse? Here he is, use him whenever you want to.'

"And quiet Uh-de! Not a word spoken, but something for my comfort to be discovered after he has gone. It is, 'Anything you want from town?' or 'Who's going to take you home?' on a trip to the Pueblo. One summer evening I said I was walking, as I sometimes do, and quick as the flash in his eye came the answer, 'Not in those shoes!'

"The women have less leisure, they, the mothers and pottery-makers, but nonetheless their thought is of me. Always they are gracious, with interest in all the little things happening to me, and many are the kindly things they do for me. Knowing my special liking for the paperbread of blue corn meal that only the older women make now, O-ne-a-po-vi always saves some for me. If there is *bu-sti-a*, a sweet bread, in the bread jar, Cah-i, remembering, adds it to the basket when I chance to be there at meal time; kindly

Cah-i, who is wife to my *Padre*. Rhubarb and carrots and corn from her garden brings O-ma-wi, who calls me sister. Ah-pa, coming to wash or clean, sometimes climbs down from the wagon seat a bit awkwardly, and I know there is something hidden under her red shawl. It has been beets, tomatoes, a melon, blue corn meal of her own grinding, once some of her pig's backbone. It was Sahn-povi who sent me venison, no small gift even here, and A-goya a box of wild plums, little things so hard to pick, for jelly. And one day Sangh-wah invited me to dinner. It was a meal prepared specially for me, corn cooked in an Indian way which I had long wanted to taste, *kapo-wano*, the fried bread I so much like, Indian pie, and celery, because I am a white woman.

"Borrowing and lending may be scorned by some, but to me they are part of being neighborly. How could I ever have enough cups for the whole village when we have a pahn-shadi, a dance over here? So Quebi always brings hers, and the big feast day coffee pot. And my benches always go to the Pueblo for feast days. It is Quebi's pink shawl I wear when I watch a sunrise ceremony, and her bed I share. And when I go to a costume party as a Pueblo woman, the best clothes of the village are at my disposal.. One Thanksgiving Day I was arrayed in much splendor; Po-te's silk dress and *ah-hi;* Quebi's silk *muto;* Sangh-wah's best shawl, O-mah-wi's buckskin boots; much silver and turquoise loaned me by all. And Tsah-pa's contribution was bangs for my wig made from his horse's black tail! Even the children are loaned to me, and my happiest hours are when I am free to play with them. Sometimes they spend a night with me, sometimes a whole wagonload comes and there is much romping in and out of the little old house. . . .

"Quebi is like a sister and I am glad her betrothal and wedding were my first such experience. They were real ceremonies, and even though I did not understand the words, the depth of it all gripped me and I knew she wanted me to share it as much as I could. It was after Povi let me put hot compresses on her knee that I felt nearer that diffident lovely woman, and her death touched me as did the whole village, with whom I wept. . . .

"But when there are personal problems to solve, or things in the

village worry me, it is to Povi-cah I go to counsel, she whom I count one of the finest of women and feel it an honor to hold as friend. Her confidence in me is held as a trust, and whether it be a house to build, or a misunderstanding to mend, she has never failed me. I told her once as I chanced to meet her in the village that I had something to talk over with her when I could come to see her. The next day she left her work, and she is a pottery maker of fame, to come over here. She thought I was worried and so she came to help me if she could, and she did."

Povi-cah is the Indian name of María, the world-famous potter. Since it was from María and Julián that Edith rented her house, she was always especially close to them and to their children. María of San Ildefonso is not only a great artist and craftswoman; she is also a wonderfully wise and rich-hearted human being. Though I have seen her seldom through the years she still has a warm smile for the child I used to be. Through her serene eyes I return to the long-ago time when life was simple and the Indian world I was just beginning to know seemed like a fairy tale. María has not had an easy life but she has walked the trail from beginning to end in beauty. It is easy to understand how much she meant to Edith.

"It matters not," Edith says at the end of her essay, "that the color of skin be different, that language be not the same, that even the gods of our fathers be known by a different name. We are people, the same kind of human beings who live and love and go on, and I find myself ever forgetting that my friends are known as Indians and I am a white woman born. Perhaps that is why we are neighbors, even down in our hearts."

Perhaps it was Edith's reticence that endeared her from the beginning to the Pueblo people, used as they are to the garrulous white man with his endless questions. She was not afraid to be silent and to let feeling flow between human beings, as it does between mesas and rivers, between trees that keep weaving the sun and the earth together. Many of her closest friendships were almost wordless. Here is a journal entry that describes how she went to San Ildefonso one day at dawn to watch a winter ceremony:

Just as I entered the plaza the door of the Deer House opened and a blanketed figure came out, followed by the dancers. The large plaza was still and unpeopled and I pressed close against the wall of an adobe house as they faced south and began the low song to which moccasined feet beat the earth with the lifted step that seems to take into the dancer strength from the mother earth. Bodies painted with black and white circles and spots I saw; red yarn fluttering on legs that moved in unison; embroidered kirtles and dangling foxskins; great collars of fir; gay feathers dancing on black hair; familiar faces intent on the prayer song. All that my eyes saw bit by bit, while the rich low tones of the song and the rhythm of the movement filled me. From the earth itself and from the house made of earth it flowed into me and I can find no word for it.

As the dancers faced the east and the blanketed leader called to the earth spirits within the center of their universe around which they were dancing, the sun rose. . . . To the sun, the life-giver, that song seemed to go, and into the plaza the sun-power to come into those bodies so concentrated on the prayer.

And then from out the house against which I leaned came that old one whom I call Sayah, which is "grandmother." I bent to her embrace with that feeling of almost awe which I experience when I realize her faith and love. We have only the few Tewa and Spanish words I know, but there is between us an understanding that needs few words. I had not seen her for several weeks, and she had been ill, which made it not an ordinary meeting, so that I was much aware of what she meant to me as I turned again to watch the dancers.

Until they had completed the square and gone into their house I watched, and then went in to warm myself by Sayah's fire. In silence we stood there, her hand in mine. In memory that dance will always be associated with Sayah, and in that region where we are and have our being, the earth-feeling which came from the dance and its background will be mingled with that which came from her.

With the men of the pueblo she had a different bond. Among the Indians whose life is so organized in community there is little

individual sharing, little chance for groping thought to be expressed. Degrees of kinship determine every relationship and custom governs almost completely the meshing of men's minds. Loneliness is something that few Pueblo Indians have learned to live with—the loneliness that every man must suffer who dares to step out of the safe framework of all he has been taught and seek his own answers to the riddle of being human. The communal life can be as lonely as any other for a man who finds his spirit imprisoned in it. In Edith these men found someone they could talk to. She had an intuitive understanding of their loneliness and never made them feel ashamed of the inward twistings of their hearts, or of their childlike sallies of sudden fun.

She had been living beside the Rio Grande only a few weeks when a middle-aged Indian came walking into the yard. A red bandana kept the bangs and sidelocks of his graying hair from blowing in the June wind. The years had begun to round his thin shoulders a little, though he was not yet old.

Joe Aguilar looked up from his work to tell her that this was Juan Estevan Roybal, Adam's father-in-law, whom she came to know by his Indian name of Chai. He clasped her hand loosely in greeting, and said haltingly, for he had very few words of English, "I look for my cows." She guessed that the cows were only an excuse and that he had really come to satisfy his curiosity about the white woman who lived at the bridge where even the Indians refused to stay because of loneliness. She invited him to come and rest before

continuing to hunt his cattle, and led the way into the little sitting room.

He walked around the room slowly, looking carefully at the pictures, the books, the pottery. Then he turned, and with a solemn face he said, "Usted muy rico"—You are very rich. This startled her, but in her meager Spanish she answered him, "Oh no, muy pobre." He laughed heartily; then at ease as though delighted to find that she knew how to joke, he sat down and lit a cigarette, forgetting all about the wandering cattle.

Chai came frequently that summer, talking little and smoking much, for he was a man of few words and fewer friendships. The rico-pobre exchange never varied; it became the pattern of similar repartee, and the play-on-words all Indians delight in. She was never quite sure what he thought of her until the day he suddenly handed her a five dollar bill. When she looked puzzled he told her, "Always you say you are poor. I bring you some money." It was probably the only cash he possessed, for his income, she knew, was both small and uncertain. It was hard to make him understand the difference between being poor, as they both were, and being destitute, but only when she promised to tell him if she were really in need would he let her give the money back.

Through the first winter and spring when she was alone beside the bridge, Chai came often from the pueblo to see if she were all right and to sit with her, especially on days when the winds were at their worst and he knew that she might be fearful.

Six years later, in the time of whirling spring wind, she wrote:

It is hard to watch Chai draw slowly toward the end, drawing deep within himself, facing alone the unknown trail. He no longer speaks, just moves his head when I touch his hand. . . . He has been known as a silent man, holding himself apart. But to me he has talked a little of himself, his worries, his thoughts, during the long hours beside the fire. He has that love of fun and laughter that is typical of the Pueblo people. . . . I realize now that the game he invented of teaching me Tewa was more than fun. It helped to bridge the gulf of racial heritage between us. It was a reaching toward each other that comes in friendship.

On the last day of April she wrote:

Chai is gone. Yesterday when I went to his house I found only his body wrapped in his old blanket. Sobs shook me, for I loved him. He no longer needed the broth and custards I had brought him. I could only gather apple and wild plum blossoms, and go back to watch through the night, remembering the years of our friendship.

This morning they took his body to the church for burial. . . . I came sobbing home along the road he had followed so many times, aware only of loss, of emptiness. Finally I looked upward toward the west, and there came like a flash the deep certainty that he had but preceded me and gone on to the mountains. I somehow knew that he was happy, and lest I make it difficult for him to do his work, I must not mourn.

I came slowly along the river road, the hereafter touching me closely for the first time. This afternoon clouds covered the clear sky of morning and a gentle rain fell. My friend has gone, but he has sent the rain. Now when the winds blow, when the rain falls gently, when special days come in the pueblo, he will be near, and I shall be happily aware of him. Without a vital friendship between us, such awareness could not exist.

NINE

*T*HERE *is an evening star with a small one quite near it. I cannot recall that before. Usually it is a solitary, lonely one. I am glad there are two together.*

One often wonders what Edith's life would have been without Tilano. He was as much a part of the little house as the river that flowed past it, as the mesas from which Edith drew her strength. In the beginning he was to me only the elderly Indian who did the chores and who was always gentle and merry with my little boys. They followed him everywhere. When he went to the well he lifted them so they could peer down it, amazed at the bright eye of water shining in the round depth, helping him hand-over-hand to lift the splashing bucket on its pulley. They followed him among the cottonwoods where the cow hid herself, and to the corrals to gather eggs, and to pick up feathers from the fanning tails of the white turkeys. But it was only little by little that he became a person to me, that I realized the dignity and wisdom beneath the banter we used with one another.

He had one of the kindest faces I have ever seen, a kindness blent with humor, a network of wrinkles that seemed not so much age as laughter. His hands, when he would take mine in greeting, had a curious dry warmth, a wiry strength. They gripped mine as lightly as a bird that perches on a finger.

At the time when the path of his life first merged with Edith's he must have been close to sixty. It was an afternoon in June of that first summer. Work had been going slowly on the west room which was to serve as store and tearoom. The man who had promised to build the corner fireplace kept delaying in the casual Indian manner. It had been hard for Edith to get used to the way things

move slowly in this land, to learn that for the Indian time has no boundaries, that every project must ripen according to seasonal rhythms and invisible inner laws.

One day when Adam came to take care of the freight he said with a note of achievement in his voice, "My Uncle Tilano is bringing the adobes for the fireplace in his wagon. Tomorrow he will come to build it."

"My Uncle Tilano" was Atilano Montoya, governor of the pueblo, and Adam's great-uncle. He came rattling over the bridge that afternoon, driving a team of white horses. After unloading the adobes he came into the house to sit awhile, to rest and talk, as Indians do so seldom, about himself.

How amazed Edith Warner was to learn that this gently aging man whose hair hung in black braids almost to his waist, had traveled far. He had crossed the ocean, had seen in his youth the great cities of history—London, Paris, Berlin, Rome. When Edith told him that she came from Philadelphia his eyes had lighted up. "Philadelphia!" he said. "I've been there. When I came back from Europe I stopped in Philadelphia for awhile. Then I came home to the pueblo."

With only a little coaxing he unfolded the story she was to hear so often. A group of Indians from San Ildefonso had gone to Coney Island one summer to display their dances. There Bostok, the animal trainer, had seen them and asked them to go with him on tour.

"Paris was the best place," Tilano said. "We stayed there a long time—maybe a month or more. The people liked us and clapped lots when we came out on the stage. When we walked on the street they crowded around us and asked, 'Are you American Indians?' Soon we learned some words of their language and could answer them."

"What did you dance?" she asked him.

"The Eagle dance," Tilano answered. "But not like here in the pueblo. There we didn't paint our bodies, and we used any kind of feathers to make the eagle wings and tail, but the French liked it."

To paint the body, to use eagle feathers would have made the dance too close to sacred ritual. Even with their bodies unpainted the dancers seem to be more than men. Their beaked headdresses

give them the piercing, penetrating look of birds. Their feathered arms become wings. So delicately they balance in their movements, they tread the hard ground as though it were made of air. The strong rhythm of the drum, the soaring voices of the chorus lift them above the earth.

What had the French people felt, Edith Warner wondered, as they watched the eagles, knowing nothing of the land to which they belonged, its heights and colors, the bare mesas, the foaming clouds, the enormous arcs of rainbow? Had Tilano, as he danced, seen the sacred mountains shining—north, south, east, west—that had guarded his childhood?

While he talked, though his mind had seemed to be far away among the years, he had been thinking about her fireplace. "I will bring a helper in the morning," he said as he rose to leave. "This dirt is no good for mud. I'll have to get some good clay from near the village." He seemed to know just the shape the fireplace needed to give the ordinary room a note of charm. In two days the job was finished, and the first fire lighted—the first of many fires that Edith and Tilano lit together—sending its sweet blue smoke upward like a plume.

I do not know exactly when it was that Tilano came to live permanently at the little house. In his own way he was as much alone as Edith. His wife had died in childbirth, in the second year of their marriage. Because of his long absence as a young man from the pueblo he was in danger of becoming rootless. Through his association with white people he had begun to know how it feels to be an individual. His integration in the communal life had been weakened. His natural sociability had already begun to find the fatal outlet in drink which often expresses the loneliness of the Indian who has become lost between two worlds. Edith was troubled about him, often deeply troubled. She felt, as only a woman could feel, that he needed the discipline of a home almost as a child needs it. His work on the little house had given him the feeling of belonging to it. He was uncle to those whose land it stood on. What wonder that she at last suggested that he come and live there instead of driving to and from his daily tasks across the bridge? What wonder that he agreed to come, saying only, "You need a man to help you."

The relationship between them is hard to define. They were not man and wife. There was a great deal of the maternal in her care for him, though he was old enough to have been her father. We used to laugh at how bossy Edith sometimes was. The child in Tilano could be stubborn and provoking as children often are. She must have given him the peace and security he needed, for he was never known to drink from that time on. She found in him the masculine strength and wisdom that kept her own life in balance, and a spirit of playfulness that had been lacking in her own serious upbringing. He is woven into her Christmas letters like the pole around which the years revolve.

Today Tilano and I went for Christmas greens . . . There were fresh deer and turkey tracks in the road and pieces of fir under a tree brushed by antlers. . . . Soon it will be Christmas Eve, and Tilano will light the little pitchwood fire out near the well house to welcome those spirits that draw near on that night. . . . Tilano and I began planting a garden on warm March days. . . . The garden where his father once worked has a special quality as well as its own charm. Even the bears came down to it this fall.

One evening as I washed dishes, the sound of a long story in Tewa reached me from Tilano's room. When I went in later, a Pueblo boy was sitting where he could hear every word and expression. Tilano looking up with his face aglow explained, "I am telling Sandy about the Shalako!" This year his great desire to see the Shalako at Zuñi has been fulfilled, and he relives the experience with each eager word. . . . Tilano is making a feather headdress, bows and arrows, tiny doll moccasins with silver buttons, for the boys and girls to whom he is a special friend. . . . Tilano's room became a winter sitting room since all day it has sunlight, a wood conserver. On stormy days I read to him while he tied parrot feathers for the dancers. The radio brought music, news, and his favorite programs. . . . Perhaps when Tilano lights the little pitch fire on this Christmas Eve, the deer whose tracks he saw at the foot of the hill will pause and watch the flames carry up into the night and across the continent our Christmas wish for peace and beauty.

I like to think how Edith's and Tilano's lives were joined, not through the physical act of becoming parents, but by the responsibility they accepted together as godparents.

A young girl from the East, seeking a period of stillness before her marriage, was directed to Edith's house in the roundabout way in which most of her contacts were made. She called herself "Peter," a name that she loved because it means rock, or stone. She stayed with Edith two months, there where the river rolls the broken stones into music, where the rocks in the hidden canyons are covered with the gay and reverent drawings of an ancient people for whom everything that lived was both holy and humorous. Later on she was joined by the young man who was to be her husband, and there, with Edith and Tilano as witnesses, they were married.

To Tilano this meant far more than a perfunctory legal act. It meant that he had in the most true and serious sense become godfather to young Peter and Earle Miller; that Edith was now their godmother. Their duty toward them both was that of spiritual guidance. Among most Indian people there is a custom that a child is initiated into manhood by a ceremonial father or mother. He is "reborn" out of the closely protected circle of his parental family into the responsible life of the tribe to which he belongs. He is made aware, by a vividly enacted symbolic drama, of the reciprocal powers of life and death, and of his own function as man in the rhythmic pattern of the cosmos.

The teaching that was given to this young couple was as private and as personal as love. Whatever Tilano could share of the great mysteries that are common to all mankind he shared with them reverently. "Those things that must not be told to white people" were never throughout his life repeated to anyone, not even to Edith, nor to those two who were their godchildren. The belief that religious truth should be imparted only to those whose hearts are prepared through slow maturing or through rigorous training is a very old one. The forces of life and germination which the Pueblo people understand so deeply, are as dangerous when handled without reverence as the energies which our own science has revealed within the atom.

"Godfather would often tease us when he heard us talking

solemnly," Peter says, "but when he *did* undertake to teach us or show us something then his manner changed. He was gruff with us and ordered us about impatiently. I wonder now if it might have been some echo of the older men's attitude in teaching novices in the kiva?"

All of us who spent any time at the river learned something from Tilano, if for some it was only the knack of letting the funny side of life exist always beside the serious. He never let us forget that laughter is of the gods, as all the Pueblos know. He was not above pinching our bottoms playfully, and because we knew him both as wise old man and ever-living child, dignified matrons that we were, we let him do it. The same voice that told Peter, as he guided her hand in gesture on the high sacred places, "Make your prayer *now*," could also tease us with wolf calls if we appeared in jeans that hugged too tightly.

During all his years by the river Tilano never failed to take his part in the ceremonial life of the village. A white man sees only the final climax of the long rituals. For the participants it means long days and nights of preparation in the kiva, hours of self-collection and concentration such as only those among us who belong to religious orders can ever know. As Tilano grew older, Edith did all she could to spare his strength for these times that demanded every fiber of physical strength in a man's being. If no one could be found to help with the usual chores Edith herself would milk and sweep new-fallen snow from paths and rooftops.

The high point of the year for San Ildefonso comes on January 22, the day of the saint's feast, and this is often the coldest part of winter. The dance begins at dawn with the calling of the Sacred Animals from the hills behind the pueblo. In order to see this part of the ceremony I and a friend once spent a night in bedrolls spread under a juniper tree at the back of Edith's house. All during the night we were aware of the moving river. Across it drifted the thin sound of chanting voices, and the faint sound of drums hid deep in the kiva. The stars above us were magnified by an icy wind until they shone like giant snow crystals.

We pried ourselves out of our beds before there seemed to be the slightest sign of morning. Edith had gotten up even earlier and had

a pot of coffee ready to warm us. After a hurried breakfast of bacon and eggs we drove to the pueblo. The Rio Grande was only a faint thread of brightness. We saw the stars wink out one by one as the outline of the mountains slowly grew firm against the eastern sky.

San Ildefonso seemed deserted. There was not even the sign of a footprint in the bare-swept plazas. The great cottonwood kept watch over the sleeping houses like an old nurse saying *Hush!* No sound came from the kiva and we felt as though even time had not waked up yet. After a while small groups of Indians appeared out of nowhere. We followed them as they went along the road that borders the Pueblo on the east.

Everyone seemed to be waiting for something, and we waited with them. How long, I wondered, could we keep from freezing? We leaned against a wall that helped to screen us from the cold morning wind. Two Indians, wrapped like cocoons in long factory-made blankets, came up beside us. They too gratefully hugged the shelter of our wall. Soon they began to talk to us, the way people do at a show before the curtain goes up. They were not San Ildefonso men, but visitors from other pueblos come to share the feast. One was from Santa Clara, only a few miles distant. The other was from Taos, sixty miles to the north. They spoke to us in English, but to one another in Spanish. The Santa Clara, the talkative one,

said they did not share each other's language. Now and then they sang little snatches of their songs. The traditional rhythms were familiar to both men, though neither knew the other's words.

The Santa Clara kept doing his best to make us feel at home. He pointed toward the curve of the nearest hill, where the tiny figure of a sentinel grew taller as the daylight brightened behind him.

"Soon they come from over there," he told us. "All kind of animal, deer, buffalo, other kind, I know not how you call him. You watch. You stay there. Soon they come." The Taos man, tall and dignified, was silent. He stood like a rock or a tree, serenely oblivious to the conversation of humans, busy with whatever thoughts his roots secretly fed on.

Suddenly close behind us the deep-throated Indian drum began to beat. A chorus of four old men came to stand at the entrance to the pueblo. They were not specially costumed; they might have been uncles or grandfathers anywhere except for their braided hair and bright headbands, their faces brown and gullied as earth. But when they began to sing our mortal hearts turned over. The need of men to live, the trust of men in the powers of life soared in their voices. They seemed to be calling upon man's kinship with the gods, and with the spirit in all living things.

Behind the chorus women and children gathered quietly. They looked toward the east, toward the morning hill, their faces uplifted in wonder and anticipation. The drum sound went forth into the hills; the deep confident male voices wove their invocation. The Santa Clara turned to us again. He almost trembled in his eagerness to explain what was happening.

"Indian sing for *all* men," he said with the deepest earnestness. "He sing for good things for this pueblo, for Indian, for all people everywhere. He sing for rain to come so summer fields grow. He sing for *everybody, everywhere*." Over and over he kept repeating this as though he thought it a thing we could hardly believe.

"Indian singing for everybody, everywhere. That what the song say. He telling them animals bring good things, not just for this pueblo; good things for everybody, for you, for me, for this people, for all people in the whole *world*."

Then we saw a plume of dark smoke swirl from the head of the arroyo high between the hills. The landscape became alive. Small figures moved among the dark dots of juniper. On the crest of the hill two Deer (who yesterday were men) lifted their antlered heads and became gods. With delicate motions they wove a zigzag trail down the slope of the hill. The Buffalo men came slowly down the arroyo, naked to the waist, painted with symbols, their great head-dresses magnificently constructed of green twigs and horn. The Antelope children pranced warily behind them, humorously clad in yellow-dyed long underwear. They were slim and small and perfectly disciplined in the manner of their going. The Hunters stood in opposing lines close to the chorus, wearing clusters of evergreen at wrist and knee. The ancient ritual began in which men renounce hatred and enmity toward all creatures, promising to take life only for the sake of need. The Hunted were invoked as though they were gods and implored to lay down their lives for the sake of all the living.

The Sacred Animals came down in a lordly way between the lines of onlookers. Small girls pushed shyly close to them. Small babies peered solemnly out from the blankets that cradled them. Little boys in faded overalls and store shirts were eager as children at the mystery of Christmas. Very tiny children hopped about in their own ecstatic circles, copying the step of the dancers with miniature accuracy.

As the divine animals passed, the waiting Indians threw pollen or sacred meal upon them. There was an atmosphere of gaiety and relief as though an ancient and vital magic had been worked once more. The sun came up in full splendor and began its journey toward the west. The dancers disappeared for awhile into the cere-monial house of the south plaza. They would come out to dance many times during the day; the plaza would fill with visitors. It would never again be so easy to believe that men could march out of the sunrise with divinity shining on their shoulders.

Peter tells me that one day as she and Edith were talking about the Buffalo Dance, it seemed to them that the power of it spread out horizontally with a tremendous reach, in contrast to the sum-mer corn dances where the power and movement is vertical, reach-

ing up into the sky and deep down into the earth. They realized, as they talked, that these long vertical lines each pass through a dancing man; he is the stitch, the link, that in that moment of dancing prayer binds earth and sky together.

After one Winter Feast in which Tilano had danced all day, Edith wrote to Peter:

Godfather looked so worn when he finally emerged. I got him home and he never even went down to see the cow. I milked and fed animals. He went to bed before nine and slept till nine the next morning. The same was true this morning. I milked so he could eat his breakfast slowly. Now he looks rested. He came in a bit ago with a rabbit that was in his trap, and now he has gone for the mail, taking his gun, hoping he'll see another.

To impersonate the gods as animals, to step out of daily life and enter a circle of time as old as the zodiac, to put off his human thought so that the thought of the Divine Ones might come streaming through him, feeling that power surge through him to the waiting touch; at day's end to go back, to become man again, to become the human self, heavy with years, exhausted as a child that has spent itself in play—this was the life that Tilano lived. This was what looked out through his wise and laughing eyes and touched in us all something older than memory.

TEN

Because I was preoccupied with my growing family—my second son was born in June of 1928, a month after Edith Warner came to live at the bridge—I scarcely noticed the transformation of the little house. I was sick a great deal of the time, and lay in bed indulging chronic sore throats and colds, rebelling against the lot of women, envying what I thought of as the freedom of men whose work took them outside the house and into adventures which I could not share. When I was well enough I used to run off to the mesas on my horse, or go to Santa Fe where my parents and girlhood friends were living, passing Edith's house again and again and never stopping.

Gradually I became aware of a difference in the little house I hurried by so often. It seemed to squat less like an ugly duckling on its sandy acre. The warm brown of unpeeled pine slabs replaced the ugly board siding. There were strings of morning-glories as blue and cool as eyes of summer sky. New windows had been cut, the old ones widened. The vines that covered the well house fell over it in a green shower. Woodbine enclosed the screen porch in a cool shade.

One afternoon I brought my children to the river on a picnic. After they had splashed and played, stubbing their bare feet on the stones, daubing each other with the sticky mud, dirty and hot as we were, Edith invited us in for tea and cookies. When we stepped in out of the raw heat I was astonished to find that the little house had become charming. Juniper wood burned in the range with the fragrance of aromatic sunshine. There was the smell of bread that had just been taken from the oven and covered with a clean cloth on the table under the kitchen window. Black pottery plates stood

upright on open shelves along one wall, with cups and saucers in terra-cotta colors from Mexico. A cabinet without doors held mixing bowls and measures and rows of spices,

The room that had been only a store had been remodeled. The counter stood inconspicuously in one end. In the opposite corner was an adobe fireplace with graduated steps on each side holding the glossy black bowls for which the San Ildefonso women are famous. There were a table and chairs for tea guests. Orange candles and red-and-black striped Chimayo squares brightened the wall; a Navajo rug covered part of the rough floor.

Since we had come as neighbors rather than anonymous customers, Edith gave us tea that afternoon, as on so many others that were to follow, in the small bed-and-sitting room that faced the east. The walls were covered with burlap that was originally made for woolsacks. Because she had almost no money at all she contrived her effects in the simplest possible way. Joe Aguilar had made tables to fit under the windows, and a desk between a pair of bookshelves against the north wall. On top of the shelves Edith had placed an Acoma pitcher and decorated bowls in tan and black, with orange-and-blue basket plaques from the Hopi country, a Navajo doll and a pair of brass candlesticks. A tiny Indian rabbit carved out of white stone sat among the pictures on the narrow shelf above the desk. On the long table among plants and books and the kerosene lamp was a pottery figure from Cochiti. The girl who sold it to her called it the "singing lady." In her journal Edith says that through the years it was this figure that became for her a symbol of woman's place in the Indian world—and of her own.

I sat on the narrow bed against the wall looking through the long sliding windows toward the Sangre de Cristos. Even Edith who saw them daily could never quite fix those mountains in her mind.

Sometimes the light makes each range stand out, casting sharp shadows on the ones behind. Occasionally when the air is very clear, there is a strange and breath-taking shining light on the green aspen leaves. At evening the twilight may run quickly from the valley, shrouding almost at once the highest peaks. Or mauve and rose

*move slowly upward, turning to blood-red on the snow above. One
morning they may be purple cardboard mountains sharpcut against
the sky. On another they will have withdrawn into themselves.
Sometimes I have watched ghost mountains with substance only
in their dark outline. It seems then as if the mountains had gone
down into their very roots, leaving an empty frame.*

The tea she served us had a thin slice of lemon floating in it
with a spicy clove. The chocolate cake that was to become a tradition for us all, from the smallest child to the world famous physicists
like Bohr and Fermi and Oppenheimer, was as tender and moist as
a spring morning. For the children there was milk, and after they
drank it they followed Tilano to the shed to stare at the cow who
had given it, to play with her calf, and to run chattering back with
an egg they had found in a hidden nest.

That first afternoon has blended in my mind with many others.
Restless, I was forever running away in search of adventure and
stimulation. One winter I drove away from the mesa in a blinding
snowstorm, and then three hundred miles south along the Rio
Grande to El Paso where the Chicago Opera Company had stopped
to perform *Thais* on a tour westward. Another summer I took flying
lessons from a pilot who was living briefly in the valley opposite
the Black Mesa—until one of the other students cracked up the
plane and killed himself and I realized that a young mother had
perhaps more important things to do.

In between times I complained that my busy household left me
no time for writing and that my husband, whose boarding-school
duties kept him busy even during the evenings and on many week
ends, gave far too little attention to his growing family.

How often I used to go to Edith, tense and frustrated, crying
against my lack of companionship, against the strict routine of the
school and what I thought of as its disparagement of everything
feminine. How little I understood then the need of adolescent boys
to live for a time in the disciplined world of men. How little I valued
the worth of my own woman's life. My long hours of solitude with
nature and with books and music yielded their harvest only many

years later. To Edith I magnified each household emergency and all the problems of relationship that inevitably arise in a small community.

She would listen as though she understood it all. Sometimes she seemed to agree, sometimes she only questioned gently. She never reprimanded nor did she ever express the envy I knew that she, the unmarried childless woman, must often feel of the secure and love-encircled life I scorned as though it were my prison. She would place a chair for me beside the kitchen table, and while we talked her hands moved endlessly about the task of daily bread. There were trays of fruit gathered at daybreak from the garden—for work in this tranquil-seeming spot began at dawn and ended long after the lamps were lighted. The garden was a quarter of a mile away. It was watered by a spring that had to be kept constantly cleared, and ditches opened to lead the thin trickle of water among the carrots and lettuce and raspberry bushes. Tilano did the heavy work, but Edith worked beside him, long hours on her hands and knees weeding and thinning the vegetable seedlings, pinching the tips of tomato plants, lovingly nursing the clumps of zinnias and marigolds.

Edith made her own jam and preserves, some from wild plum and chokecherry that grew in thickets along the ditches near the pueblo. Each autumn she canned dozens of jars of fruit and vegetables. She baked her own bread, relying as little as possible on supplies that would have to be ordered from Santa Fe and sent out by train. Her washing was usually done by women from the pueblo. Every drop of water was hauled from the well in buckets and Tilano had to be reminded to keep them filled. The lamps must be cleaned daily and the wicks kept trimmed. The big refrigerator burned kerosene and too often it went on strike and poured black smoke over everything. Dishes had to be washed and rinsed in pans filled from kettles on the stove.

She was always too thin, thin as a reed by a salt marsh. When I put my arms around her in greeting I could feel the hips and shoulders as bony as a boy's. There was often a look of strain about her mouth until she broke into one of her pixie-like smiles. Some have felt that her life was so austere, so dedicated that there could

be no place in it for gaiety, yet her closest friends were those with whom she could be playful—from Tilano to the youngest child of the pueblo. It was when she smiled that I realized her face which had seemed so plain at first was really heart-shaped. Her firm chin came to a point like a resolute valentine. She could never have lived through her strenuous days if she had not learned to balance activity with moments of quiet and of pure joy. She records such moments again and again in the pages typed from her journal, until one feels that in them lay the secret she most desired to share and which she found so hard to express, even to those of us who thought we knew her best.

I ran away today, so sick I was of the kitchen and everlasting food. Constant walls and a roof do something to me at any time and when the aspens turn golden, I seethe inside until finally I revolt and leave everything.

The sun was just above Baldy when I walked to the Pueblo for the old white horse, but by the time I reached the trail leading to the top of Shumo, it was halfway up the heavens. Shumo has a round knoll on its top which is the highest spot in the valley, and I had to be on top of my world today. All the beauty of the valley lay below me. Beyond were mesas reaching westward to the Jemez with its masses of golden aspens. The whirring of a bird overhead and the rushing of the river far below me were the only sounds. If I were a leader of people on such a day I would send them out alone into the open.

This morning when I stood on the river bank, the sun was making all golden the edge of the clouds in the west. There was a blue sky above Shumo, but snowflakes were blown thick and fast from the canyon until they hid the mesas. As they shut out the world and made for me a hushed place in their midst, I was very near the source of things.

Yesterday when I woke there were clouds in the east and I was happy . . . Later the winds blew them away and I doubted. But by noon the snow had come and it fell until the earth was thickly

covered. When darkness came, I went out into it—that softly falling whiteness in the hush of the night. This morning all was heavy with snow and from it rose a white veil about the foot of the mesa. I was alone in a world of snow and I was conscious only of what came to me from it.

This is a day when life and the world seem to be standing still— only time and the river flowing past the mesas. I cannot work. I go out into the sunshine to sit receptively for what there is in this stillness and calm. I am keenly aware that there is something. Just now it seemed to flow in a rhythm around me and then to enter me —something which comes in a hushed inflowing. All of me is still and yet alert, ready to become part of this wave that laps the shore on which I sit. Somehow I have no desire to name it or understand. It is enough that I should feel and be of it in moments such as this. And most of the hatred and ill will, the strained feeling is gone— I know not how.

No, it is not what Ouspensky experienced when he was drawn by the waves into them, becoming all—mountain, sea, sky, ship. I am I and earth is earth—mesa, sky, wind, rushing river. Each is an entity but the essence of the earth flows into me—perhaps of me into the earth. And to me it is more than a few seconds' experience. Nor is it any longer strange but natural, not ecstatic but satisfying. The detail of life becomes the scaffolding.

Christmas was always one of her busiest periods. There were gifts to be made for her friends in the pueblo and on the mesa; boxes of cookies were packed, tiny jars of plum or chokecherry jelly made gay with Christmas wrappings. Evergreen boughs were gathered for those who lived in faraway cities, small toys were chosen and wrapped for brown-skinned and white-skinned children. During one of these hectic seasons she writes:

Even in these rushed days there is such peace between. There are moments when two eagle feathers can fill me with joy; when the last rays of the sun touch my forehead as I stand by the kitchen

door; when the outline of To-tavi is marked in rhythm against a clear western sky; when even the wind is part of it all. Surely such moments do something to me. If not, it is because I hide beneath the pettiness. I have no apparent goal. I only know that I am living a day at a time as I feel the way.

February usually brought an interval of peace. Christmas was long past; the San Ildefonso winter feast was over. The few visitors who came were friends with whom Edith could relax and talk about books or magazines she had little time to enjoy at other seasons. Even the earth seemed to be resting. The next summer's leaves were still folded tight in their sheaths along the twigs of the cottonwoods. Winds escaped only briefly from their caves. The river moved quietly, its spring torrents locked in the ice and snow of the high mountains. During such rare peaceful days Edith makes these notes:

Today the sun shines here, but the clouds hang low on the Sangre peaks and beyond Shumo. Again I have touched the fringe of the unknown and been drawn to it, not by my seeking, which is the only real way.

As I worked . . . there came without warning a flowing into me of that which I have come to associate with the gods. I went to the open door and looked up at the mountains with something akin to awe. It forced me out into the open where I could look up to those sacred high places on which humans do not dwell. Then it left me— perhaps to return to those sacred places.

I had almost forgotten how to lie curled on the ground or here on my couch, content just to look and feel and enjoy the thoughts that come. Rushing with things to be done crowding is such a waste of living. There need to be hours of this.

It is almost impossible to imagine how she managed to find these moments of quiet in the midst of her busy life. For a long time she had the job of reading the river gauge on the bridge that measured

the fluctuating stages of water for the flood control program of a government agency. To do this she must climb down the side of one of the supporting abutments, sometimes just over the swirl of a springtime flood. I remember how for two or three months each spring she suffered acute hay fever from the juniper pollen flying at the very time that the garden must be planted, often in days of seething wind. Her only times of rest came in late fall and early winter when the garden had been put to bed and visitors came seldom, when the solitude she loved remained for days unbroken. So harassed was she in summer by the constant flow of people that she sometimes sent those she loved away from her, knowing that we would understand her need for self-collection.

I heard a visitor ask her once if she were ever frightened.

"By what?" she wondered in surprise.

"By the solitude," the city woman imagined.

"Never," Edith answered without hesitation. "Only people frighten me."

The people who frightened her were those who guard themselves in trivial words to which she could never find an easy way of responding, and with these she had to deal increasingly as time went on and the road past her house became more traveled.

"There was a time," she writes, "when I sought to put out of my life or go away from those humans who irritated me or disturbed the rhythm of my being. Now that I have come this far on the way, I know that the only way is to become impervious to the irritation." In a later note she corrects herself and says, "I am dubious. Perhaps it is I who am out of rhythm."

In 1934 she was able to add a separate guest house built of adobe with a sheltered portal that faced the curve of the river. Here those seeking rest for tired bodies and more often for tired minds could come for a few weeks of quiet and solitude. Partly because she was so busy, partly because she had such faith in the healing quality of silence, Edith left her visitors very much to themselves. There were no modern conveniences. A pitcher and basin stood on the wash-stand beside the bed. Tilano kept the pitchers filled with water and laid sticks of piñon upright in the corner fireplace. Edith would light the fire for the weary guest and then smile and go away. At

night each must walk, lantern in hand, along the stony path through the fragrant juniper shadow to the adobe privy that stood above the riverbank. Sometimes a coyote would cry, an owl call softly. The river rushed like a wind over its stones.

It was the simplicity of her life that we all envied, few of us realizing at what cost that simplicity was achieved.

"That month in her little guest house was one of the perfect experiences of my life," a friend says in a letter. "I think I have never known anyone so quiet and reserved who became so much a part of one's life and thinking—what priceless gifts of the spirit Edith had to give and how generously she gave them."

"Edith loved the simile, 'a flute of the gods,'" her goddaughter tells me. "She was always trying to keep herself clear and her heart right so that she could be a perfect instrument. She was as close to being completely free of self as anyone I have known.—And yet she too had her struggles, up to the very end."

She barely hints at her own struggles in the dozen or so typed pages from her journal which were all she was content to share with other eyes—and there are no more entries after February of 1935.

She begins in September 1929:

It is a feast day at San Ildefonso. I am glad, so glad to be alive and here, with the past year of adjustment and illness only a memory. It is a fall day with great clouds and soft breezes from the south— the kind that draws my soul a-tiptoe.

Perhaps part of this exultant mood is due to what I saw this morning. As I went to the pueblo I recalled my first September Corn Dance. I had come on horseback from the mountains and stayed overnight. The babies I had held then were dancing today and from the shade of the big cottonwood I watched them. Just beyond me were the chorus and the dancers with an old two-storied house and the Black Mesa as a background. There were no cars, no curious tourists to mar the solemnity—only Indian children who belonged. Here where I know each one, it is faces I see; attitude I note; feeling I catch. The words of the song, the gestures of the chorus, the figure of the dance has no literal meaning for me, but I felt the intangible

*that permeated them. It was not similar to those moments when all
of me seems drawn upward by the beauty of the night or the hills.
It was more what one might feel in a Presence. And somehow there
in that plaza guarded by the old, old cottonwood, the last dregs were
drained from me. I can endure anything if now and then come such
hours.*

*My eyes are still seeing dancers, my ears still hearing the beat of
the tombé and the rise and fall of voices. I should not have left whatever business there might have been, but when Awa asked me to go
to Santa Clara this morning, I locked the door and went. I needed it.*

*Always the eagle dance fills me with something of the sky. Today
I watched the dancers from such close proximity that I saw leg-
muscles move. As I watched, oblivious of chorus and onlookers,
there came something of the gods to those hovering, circling eagles.
Then from a housetop I looked down at the whirling, swooping
dancers. Into the heights they took me—up where the god-powers
dwell. That was a dance for the soul.*

*I told Quebi that if I were an Indian, I should want to be a man
to dance as the men do. My body still seems to whirl and turn with
them. But as I watch it in memory, the dance revolves around the
women, the women who softly, lightly, slowly, with feet scarcely
lifted from the ground, form the center of the movement. Pueblo
women are like that—soft laughter, low voices, quiet steady movements, holding their men and their children through the life dance.*

*Twice within this week I have seen what must be meant only
for the delight of the gods. I chanced to look up from my reading
a bit ago, and went flying out to the river bank. My carved foothill
was a shining thing of beauty. No artist could capture the gold that
bathed it with wonder and set it apart. And while I looked in awe,
from its earth-hold rose slowly a new color—a cloak of mauve only
less bright than the gold that with a caressing movement wrapped
itself about my golden hill. Only then could I look to faraway purple
mountains and the Mesa which was quite black against a clouded
sky. When I looked back to the hill the magic was gone. Can such
beauty be and then not be? I think the gods must have taken back
to themselves that godmade color—perhaps to paint themselves for*

an approaching ceremony. And I know that some of it came to stay with me.

The winds tried hard yesterday to blow away the snowfilled clouds . . . finally with a last great blast they went back to their caves and were still. All night and all day the clouds have hung low. . . . And from them have come rain and hail and snow to the thirsty earth. I had forgotten that snowflakes could fall so gently to make a curtain that shut out the world. Perhaps never before had I known snow like this, for the Pueblo people have been calling it to come.

Today they are dancing the Turtle dance—all the men and boys in ceremonial costumes with great collars of fir, with turtle shells tied on knees, and with gourd rattles to mark the rhythm of the song. It is a long song that calls the rain to come and the earth to yield—the same that those ancients prayed when they lived in cañons and on mesas. And perhaps then, as today, the snow fell in such stillness to the waiting earth. It seemed as though the gods came in the sky as great eagles who gave the soft white down from their breasts. It was in the hair of the dancers and on the breast of the earth—sent by the gods to those who forget not how to ask for it.

Just now as I watched the ever-changing beauty, I saw a cloud pass over the earth on long grey stilts of rain. And then as I looked I saw its shape and knew that over the pueblo moved the Thunder Bird. With wings outspread he slowly passed, broad tail sweeping the thirsty earth. Down from his breast fell feathers of rain and out from his heart the lightning flashed its message to the people that the gods never forget. Thunder roared from his long black beak and all earth sounds were hushed. He has gone, leaving only his mark on the land, but I still see his broad wings stretched, and the white rain-feathers dropping from his breast. And any fear, lingering from those childhood days when I, unafraid, was made to fear lightning, has gone. Did it not come from his heart? If it should seek me out or find me wandering in its path, would it not take me back with it? I should not mind going so much if I could look down on beauty like earth's today.

I have been sitting here looking at the peaked ceiling of two gray and one brown, one rough and one smooth board—the only roof for which I have any affection—wondering why such heights and depths have been given me. There are days when I question the gods. And then come the things that make me catch my breath. There are moments when this crude house, my little pottery singing woman, my books and pictures are filled with something that sends out to me peace. Is it because of an ancient prayer that color and form and movement have come to mean so much more, or is it that the years bring an increased vision—no, a more understanding vision? Is it a natural gift that accompanies maturity, or is it a gift of the gods?

I am glad that the years of adjustment are over and that there has come to me this new relationship with all of earth. I know that I was never so aware of the river and the trees; that I never walked so eagerly looking for the new wild things growing. I know that I have had to grow sufficiently—no, to cast off enough of civilization's shackles so that the earth spirit could reach me.

This morning I stood on the river bank to pray. I knew then that the ancient ones were wise to pray for peace and beauty and not for specific gifts except fertility which is continued life. And I saw that if one has even a small degree of the ability to take into and unto himself the peace and beauty the gods surround him with, it is not necessary to ask for more.

ELEVEN

HOW DIFFERENT my own life was in the small community
we called Los Alamos. Two thousand feet above the river, more than
seven thousand feet above the level of the sea, our mesa might have
been a different world. My house, close to the edge of the canyon
that borders the mesa to the north, was two-storied, built of log and
stone. The forest was at my back door, pine trees, some of them three
feet in diameter, in which the summer wind made constant music.
I had a small lawn and a garden of delphiniums, marigolds and
zinnias, even a miniature pool made of an old bathtub in which
goldfish swam and a water lily grew. There were wisteria vines
over the window and a scarlet climbing rose by the front door. The
children slept on a screened porch shaded by honeysuckle vines,
and a crab-apple tree under which a family of skunks used to keep
festival on moonlit autumn nights.

The school grew and many of the young masters married. The
wives took turns at giving informal supper parties. Several of the
men were musical; one sang; another played the violin. I often
accompanied the singing of Bach chorales and Christmas carols and
helped with practice for the Gilbert and Sullivan operetta which
was produced each spring. My children grew and became amusing
and companionable. They peer now from the pages of my own
journal in moments of tenderness and laughter. The typed pages
I have kept run through the same years as Edith's. Like hers, they
are filled with a love of nature, yet I realize now, that with only
the distance of a few miles between us, we saw the world through
wholly different eyes.

"August, 1929. The north window opens toward the canyon, by night a wild dark place. I can hear cattle bells that snap across the darkness from the mesa on the other side. Birds utter faint, far cries. The mountain has disappeared into darkness and the sky is only paling light above. Now the cattle bells rattle past the west windows. They sound like the voices of animate creatures seeking each other in the darkness.

"From my north window I can see a storm coming down from the mountains. The white mist spills over the arm of the mountain. I can hear the heavy rain beating across the canyon. Thunder rolls in antiphonal effect from peak to peak. The wind surges down from the mountains, spills into the canyons, wells up with an added strength against the house. The green curtains flatten themselves against the window as if they were hunted things. After all this frenzy of preparation at last only a few silly drops spill onto the metal roof of the garage. Was the storm only a pretense? No, the mist I thought was thinning has gathered again. It is marching nearer like the gray shadow of an army. A swift flame leaps across it and crashes into thunder. Now the rain wrestles with the wind for mastery in the tree tops. It pours down from the clouds like a river. How strange the trees look, like ghosts caught in a gray curtain. The rain is all between and among them. It is a world of the newly dead groping in a purgatory without color. Humans creep now beneath whatever little shelter they can, and whisper and touch cold hand to hand till the storm is past. They dare not be caught out when the rain gods march.

"February, 1931. It is colder tonight and the clouds have lifted. That which this afternoon was a mist, as soft and white as breath on frosty mornings, thin, formless, weightless, a fairy fog, has gone up into the sky. It has thickened around the moon like cream clotted on a pan of milk. A yellow light glows upon the snow. The mountains are faintly yellow. Trees shed faint blue shadows upon the snow, there are round pools of blackness south of each tree where no snow fell, or if it fell, it melted quickly off into the warm, moist earth.

"February, 1932. (A recollection in winter.) I can see the slopes

of Redondo as we started up, steep and shaggy with ancient fallen trees. The thin sunlight was something very old and faded that trickled through the heavy shadows of the trees still standing. I think of the myriads of violets growing among the rocks on the higher treeless slopes. How bitter and cold and windy it was, and yet there were violets. I remember after we came down again, the long trail along the thread of water before we reached our camp, my unspeakable weariness, the bathing my tired feet in the icy stream; then falling for a moment of bliss into deepest sleep.

"JULY, 1932. I watch from my window the rain falling out of the center of heaven, hardly veiling the mountains that are flooded with the light of evening. A double rainbow is the arch of the stage. The theater, where I sit, is dim. The mountains live and shine in glory. The field this side of the fence has been planted to sunflowers, deep, sturdy green, not yet in blossom. The poplar tree sings in all its leaves. Oh moment of wonder for which the whole of life might be lived!

"NOVEMBER, 1932. The baby sits on the bed, sleepy and hungry, waiting for his supper, knowing beyond the shadow of doubt that he will be fed. He is so young, so isolated from this world and all its trouble, its aspiration, its bitter failure, its tremendous courage to begin again.

"FEBRUARY, 1933. Allen has gone across the fields to let Buffy out of the kennels. He is not yet five and sings and skips as he goes, songs without words, sounds of delight. He is breaking the ice on the roadside ditch, pounding it with his little shovel. Teddy comes to join him, but the seven-year-old has work to do and I send him back to it. 'Shades of the prison house!'

"MARCH, 1933. Today the air is so heavy with dust that not even the Jemez mountains a few miles away are visible. There are no mountains in the world, only the gaunt trees like shadows in the dusty air, and a sullen wind moves blindfolded among the trees.

"JULY, 1934. Today I thought, watching the thin shower of rain falling at the end of the mesa, Oh why doesn't it fall here? And then rejoiced that some little thirsty spot on these mesas was getting it even if it wasn't this one. It's all the same earth, I thought. Anywhere that rain falls is healing for the earth.

"August, 1934. The moon last night made a porpoise or a dolphin out of black cloud and haloed it with silver. Today is the most shining green and gold early autumnal day. I walked down the mesa at noon and heard the wind like the swish of long taffeta skirts in the corn. The tassels of the corn were deep maroon. I sat at the edge of the growing field of winter rye and saw it moved by the quick wings of little birds. Coming home I found wild white flowers like tiny moonflowers in the grass, with an exquisite delicate perfume like petunia but far more subtle.

"July, 1937. I stopped in the baby's room a moment to listen to him sleeping and as he lay and breathed so softly I remembered the winter week when he was so ill and I so frightened, and how in the night I would think I could not hear him breathe, and would go beside him and listen, that breath so troubled and so faint. How lightly strung upon life we are, like beads upon a string.

"The thunderstorm has passed. The mesa is still in shadow, but the horizon is bright. There are new curtains at the window, homespun, the color of the afterglow upon the Sangre de Cristo. There is the smell of hot gingerbread baking for supper. Soon we will sit down at the table, I and the husband and sons for whom I prepare the daily bread. We will break our bread carelessly, we who have never had to worry about where our next meal is coming from. It is likely that we will forget to give thanks, taking life so for granted.

"But I think: The sun shines upon us now. Eat and drink deep, husband and sons. Grow strong. For all life is a debt that must one day be repaid. From those who have received much, much will be demanded. There may be darkness to the extent that we have received light. In the dark time life will not give to us as we are used to be given to. But the courage to live will be demanded of us still. Eat and drink deep, oh husband and sons."

Only a little of the shadow side of our lives is preserved in these journal entries, for like Edith, I long ago discarded the fretful pages that dealt with my inner struggles and discontents. The rest has blown away with the chaff, or forms part of the compost at the roots of time.

TWELVE

LITTLE BY LITTLE the noise of the river changed, the river of time upon which our lives had been carried so peacefully. The stain of war began to mingle with its current. The events that uprooted us came suddenly in the end, yet for years there were premonitions. They echoed deep within us, almost unnoticed, like the rolling of a pebble, the trickle of dust grains, the faint quiverings that precede a landslide.

In 1938 I made this entry in my journal:

"Violent nature intruded stubbornly on the calm of daily life last night. The music we tried to hear was made inaudible by static worse than I have ever heard on the radio. A newscast explained that a tremendous electro-magnetic hurricane had taken place about one o'clock the preceding night, effectively blotting out all short-wave communication for several hours. It was the largest such storm ever to be recorded. A coyote apparently caught in a trap not far away wailed and shrieked in spirals of sound that sent shivers up and down our spines and took us back to our primitive history when men's houses were fragile islands of safety against which the wilderness beat like threatening waves. In the middle of the night I felt my bed rock and tremble gently as though in the beginning of an earthquake. Poor earth, I thought, so harassed tonight by nature and by man, bombarded by electric particles from space, torn and bruised by man's devices of war, what wonder that you should dream of shaking loose this plague that has fastened itself upon you, and tremble as you dream?"

During the spring of 1940 we hung upon our radios listening to the saddening reports of the invasion of France. Far away as we were, we felt the ancient wounds begin to open. I remember how

desperately I tried at first to escape from awareness of what was happening, to take my children's hands and flee beyond the reach of history. On June 30 my journal says:

"We got clear away into an almost inaccessible canyon, and then miraculously all the cares and strains of the past weeks began to drift away like the network of ripples on water when the wind ceases. Here in the canyon were no books of opinion, no newspaper headlines, no blare of radio with its undercurrent of panic. There were only the great sky and the ancient rocks, the stir and surge of wildflowers blooming, the sound of the rippling brook. There were beaver dams, and the mirror-like water spread out under tangled thickets, the unhurried wise old fish moving in the water, dew on the tall weeds and grass, birds calling and hurrying, the footprints of bear and mountain cat on the trail, masses of wild strawberries under tall rock shadows. How far away war seemed. Time stood still in this great moment of peace and beauty."

The news of Pearl Harbor was like a dream at first. We had eaten our midday dinner at the Lodge, the school's great dining hall with the portal that faced across lawns and gardens to the east. It was a sunny Sunday afternoon. The air was warm and brilliant. The valley below the mesa brimmed with light. Whoever first heard the startling news over his radio spread the word quickly. War had been for so long only a tangle of words in the air around us it seemed hardly possible that it could actually touch our lives.

By February of 1942 the academic headmaster, Lawrence Hitchcock, then a major in the Army reserves, was called to active duty. My husband became acting headmaster and in addition to his load of teaching was harassed by the problem of finding replacements for those of the staff who were leaving at the end of the year to enter the Armed Forces. He worked late into the night those months, and when he came to bed tossed and turned restlessly. I listened, like all anxious wives, to the speeding tempo of his heartbeat that seemed to echo the speeding tempo of our days.

One morning in the spring of 1942 I walked to the edge of the canyon and sat dreaming for awhile under the branches of a fir tree. The air was gossamer. A haze of subdued light lay over rock and tree. I watched thunderheads build up in the north over Tsacoma,

the sacred mountain. A tiny spider spun a web from the twig of a barberry to my knee and back again.

But roughly upon the edge of peace that day an airplane droned, circling back and forth among the clouds, from the river to the mountain, south along the flowing hills on the horizon, out of sight, and then suddenly back again. It flew low, methodically. The sunlight glinted from its silvery structure. It was then I first knew without doubt that a time was ending. Not even here on these mesas was isolation possible. We too were vulnerable to change. The narrow trails cut in the ancient rock could not be defended against the invading future.

On the first of May we waked to the sound of an extraordinary wind. The sky that had been limpid at daybreak darkened. The sun was muffled, though there were no clouds. The bright air was choked with dust that stung our faces and burned our eyeballs. We women were too restless that day to stay alone in our houses. Each went to seek some neighbor for reassurance, and as we walked we leaned against the wind like ghosts. Tarpaper ripped from roofs whirled past our windows. Sheds were overturned. Paths and doorways were blocked by fallen trees. Before it died at evening the wind cut a wide swath of destruction across mountain and mesa.

When I next rode on the trail up the Guaje ridge northwest of Los Alamos I became for the first time in my life almost hopelessly lost. Trees lay scattered as though spilled from a giant matchbox. Great roots had been flung upward out of pits of earth. Picking my way through the ruined landscape I lost all sense of direction. My confused mare balked and trembled till at last I got off and led her. I knew that for the animal's sake, if not my own, I must not panic. I talked to her gently and turned from time to time to lay my hand on her sweating neck in reassurance. At the peak of despair I stumbled across a shattered root. Exposed in the gaping earth shone a black piece of carved obsidian. That unexpected pattern of symmetry could only have been formed by the hand of man. I picked it up and held it in my hand, an ancient spearhead, and suddenly felt that I was not alone. An age-old human instinct for finding order in the midst of chaos came to my rescue. In a few moments I found myself back on the homeward trail.

Early the next December—a year after Pearl Harbor to the day—the faculty and boys were called to the "Big House" after dinner for a special meeting. I had to stay at home. Not long before, I had bought some sage-green material to make new curtains for our living room. They were almost ready to be hung, so while I waited I measured and pleated the edges where the drapery hooks were to be inserted. Something was going on; I had no idea what. Men in military uniform had been coming and going among us since spring but their presence was never explained. Airplanes had continued to fly over.

The meeting did not last long yet it seemed hours before I heard footsteps running. A door slammed and my ten-year-old son who had been looking forward for years to becoming a Los Alamos student like his brothers, burst in the front door, ran past me to his room, and big as he was, threw himself down on his bed and began to cry. He was unable to explain what the matter was and I had to wait for my husband to come and tell me what he had known for weeks. The school would have to close.

At midterm in February the boys were to be sent home. At first the Government had requested that no explanation be given, but Mr. Connell insisted that he must have an official notice from the military authorities that this action was necessary for the war effort. A formal letter from Mr. Stimson was framed and hung outside the director's office and a copy of it went out in the letter to the parents.

Under the stimulus of crisis, the boys were put through the full year's course of study in the remaining weeks. The senior boys, among them our eldest son, received their diplomas and were allowed to enter the college of their choice. The younger boys transferred to other schools. At Christmas I moved with our youngest boy to Taos where my mother and my brother's family were then living. My husband and the older boys stayed on at Los Alamos until the term was ended.

Even before I left, bulldozers moved in, and other weird machines roared up and down digging ditches for the foundations of future buildings. Everything was conducted in an element of extreme haste and mystery. Civilian visitors were conducted on tours of inspection everywhere, even through our homes. One day I recog-

nized Dr. Ernest Lawrence, whom my husband and I had met one summer in California. He seemed strangely diffident when I questioned him about our mutual friends, and broke away as quickly as possible from my attempts at conversation.

Another afternoon I was introduced to a young-looking man by the name of Oppenheimer. Cowboy boots and all, he hurried in the front door and out the back, peering quickly into kitchen and bedrooms. I was impressed, even in that brief meeting, by his nervous energy and by the intensity of the blue eyes that seemed to take in everything at a glance, like a bird flying from branch to branch in a deep forest. I had no idea then who he was. Later my husband, who taught the sciences, math and chemistry and physics, told me that Oppenheimer was renowned for research into the structure of the atom. We both knew that Dr. Lawrence had developed the cyclotron at Berkeley and this led us to suspect that the mysterious project for which our school had been taken over had something to do with atomic research. What this had to do with war I, at least, was too innocent to imagine. We were too impressed with the emphasis upon secrecy to mention the names of these men to anyone. Rumors of course blew back and forth like tumbleweeds in a high wind, especially among our friends in Santa Fe, and we played the game by inventing fabulous fairy tales about what the Army might be up to. Perhaps, we said, they might be planning a submarine base in the pond where the ducks swam, and a secret passage would connect it with the Rio Grande!

We played the game and hid the soreness in our hearts, going on with our own lives as best we could. My husband taught one year in a California school, but we could not be happy there among the unfamiliar seasons and in an academic life so conservative and different from the adventurous background we were used to. We moved back to New Mexico and my husband opened a school in Taos which was modeled as closely as possible upon Los Alamos. It was too much like trying to breathe life back into a dead body. The times had changed. The war was still upon us and no one could dream what new patterns might be emerging. At the end of a year he gave up the venture and tried one line of work after another so that we would not have to leave New Mexico.

THIRTEEN

Through Edith Warner's years at the bridge the pressure of human life kept gnawing away at the isolation of the plateau. West of the bridge the road had been straightened and graded. A new road up the steep side of a cliff replaced the old one that used to wind through the canyon, crossing the stream more than twenty times on the way to Los Alamos. An improved road was built into the Valle Grande where only herders once wandered with their sheep in summer. In the autumn of 1941 railway crews began to tear up the tracks of the D. & R. G. narrow-gauge railroad. The little train we knew affectionately as the "chili line" would run no longer. The sound of busy trucks roaring over the bridge replaced the bright whistle of the engine. The road to Santa Fe had gone through several stages of improvement, and until the war the number of tourists who found their way to the tearoom at Otowi grew steadily greater.

During the first years of the war Edith had found it almost impossible to keep going. Gas rationing meant fewer visitors and more difficulty getting the supplies she needed. Should she put aside "selfish desires," she asked herself? Go back to the outside world and a war job?

In the midst of her confusion—this was late in 1942—she learned that the Los Alamos Ranch School was closing. A construction company moved in with all kinds of heavy equipment. A fence was thrown round several thousand acres on the plateau; the whole area was converted into an Army post and closely guarded.

The civilians who came to work at Los Alamos were also closely guarded and apparently never allowed to leave the mesa. But in the early spring of 1943 the civilian head of the project began com-

ing down once a week with his wife to Edith Warner's house for dinner. Curiously enough he turned out to be a man she knew. Looking a little like the slim and wiry hero of a Western movie, in blue jeans and cowboy boots and spurs, he had stopped at the little house years ago at the beginning of a packtrip. Edith had given him tea and a slice of the magical chocolate cake that seemed to compel whoever tasted it to come back for more. This man too had come back. There was something about him that she liked. His senses were alert as some creature of the woods. He had a poet's face, with eyes as blue as gentians and a mouth that was at the same time firm and a little wistful. She learned that he was a professor of physics at a California university.

He had known and loved the plateau since the summer of 1922 when he took a pack trip from Frijoles into the Valle Grande—this must have been only a short while before Edith came to stay in the canyon with the Boyds. Later he and his brother bought a ranch in the Pecos Valley, high on the east side of the mountains and returned many times for camping trips to the Pajarito country. It was in the summer of 1937 that he first stopped at Edith's. In 1941 he brought his wife to meet her—like so many other young men who as boys had fallen under the spell of the little house and wanted to share it with those they loved.

It was not until 1945, after the atomic bombs had been exploded at Hiroshima and Nagasaki, that she could tell us this was Robert Oppenheimer.

It was he who had suggested Los Alamos to the Army as a possible site for the development of the bomb. It was the merest chance that he knew of the existence of such a place and that he had the intuitive mind to sense its possibilities.

"Ever since the discovery of nuclear fission, the possibility of powerful explosives based on it had been very much in my mind, as it had that of many other physicists," he admitted later. "We had some understanding of what this might do for us in the war and how much it might change the course of history."

They had some understanding too of what it might do against us. The race was against time, they believed. The knowledge that the Germans were experimenting with the military uses of atomic fission was the spark that ignited our own fierce effort.

This effort, as Oppenheimer tells us, had at first been scattered and fragmentary. Science has always depended upon the cooperation of many minds; in this perhaps lies its real hope for us all. Wartime restrictions were making intercommunication increasingly difficult. A central laboratory was needed where extreme secrecy somehow could be combined with the utmost freedom for men to share their experience with one another. Through Oppenheimer's acquaintance with the locale, Los Alamos was selected out of several relatively inaccessible areas in New Mexico as the one the Army believed most appropriate for the site of this laboratory. It was remote; housing already was available, and the setting was beautiful. This last was a factor that seemed important to Oppenheimer, for he knew the quality of the men whom he hoped to induce to work there, and was sure they would respond to surroundings that stretch and enrich the spirit.

Oppenheimer persuaded the military authorities to let small groups of men and women come down from "the Hill" for dinner at the little house by the river. Caught up as he now was in the whirlpool of war, the furious plans to construct a deadly weapon, the impossible and often agonizing decisions that must be weighed and implemented from day to day, and often from moment to moment, he never forgot that the heart must have its nourishment. He sensed that uprooted people had a particular need that these hours at Edith's house could fill. Perhaps from his own experience he knew

that those whose daily thoughts were involved with techniques of destruction would find healing for their divided spirits at the place-where-the-river-makes-a-noise.

The security regulations, as he himself has observed, were really fantastic. Families were supposed to come with their husbands if they wanted to, but they were not allowed to leave. Telephone calls were monitored. It was illegal to mail a letter except in the authorized drops and all incoming and outgoing mail was censored. Drivers' licenses were all made out under fictitious names. The post was guarded and the laboratory was guarded within the post. No wonder that through the years of tension there were many people at Los Alamos who felt that only their evenings at Edith Warner's kept them human.

One and sometimes two groups came down nearly every night. Places were often booked for weeks in advance. There even came to be a kind of rivalry between those who had regular places on the list, and those who were seldom able to get there.

The meals that Edith served were always simple: a stew flavored with herbs on big terra-cotta Mexican plates; *posole,* an Indian dish made of parched corn; lettuce in a black pottery bowl; fresh bread; a sweet tomato relish, watermelon pickle, spiced peaches or apricots; a dessert of raspberries. Tilano served and sometimes joked a little, his long braids swinging as he poured hot coffee into big pottery cups. Edith kept busy in the kitchen, moving swiftly and quietly between stove and table in her deerskin moccasins, managing everything without fuss or hurry, though she had worked since dawn, and dishwashing, with all the water heated in kettles on the stove, would go on long into the night. She knew that for most of her guests this was the only respite from the tension in which their days were spent. For her it was a war job beyond her wildest expectations.

What this time was like no one can tell better than she does in the third of her Christmas letters:

New Year's day of this historic 1945 held no hint of the atomic era. There were no blasts from the Pajarito Plateau making discord in the song of the chorus as I sat in the sun on an old portal at San Ildefonso. Teen, just past two, watched the dancers with me and

later demonstrated the steps of the little deer. The only indication of war was the absence of his father and the other young men.

During January I rested and learned to milk, but the pueblo prepared for San Ildefonso's feast day on the 23rd. It was the time for the ceremonial Buffalo dance, and once again I took Tilano over to the house where he and all the dancers make themselves ready. On the morning of the fourth day they went into the hill before dawn to await the haunting song of the chorus. I leaned against an old adobe house as the deep drum tones rolled and the song called the men who dance as godly animals. For hundreds of years a chorus has called and a line of women waited at the foot of the hill—waited to touch these men and take into themselves that intangible spiritual power sometimes attained by human beings. As the song reached its climax a long gray plumed serpent of smoke rose from the hilltop and spread over the pueblo. From between the hills came the leader, the hunters, the Buffalo lady and men. From over the hills came Deer and Antelope and Mountain Sheep. All came to the foot of the hill where the women waited to touch them, where the chorus waited to accompany them to the plaza with exultant song.

Tilano, who has always been a Deer, became the leader this year. Babies I had held were grown up enough to be Antelope and Sheep. Tomacita and Facundo were Buffalo, and their son slept in his cradle in the ceremonial house where they danced. These human bonds make contact for me, so that the snow falling softly and quietly on the earth, on deer antlers and buffalo manes and curved sheep horns, was significant.

Pruning was finished but the first peas had not been planted when Joe came to tell me that his father, Ignacio, had gone on his last journey to the hills. It was Ignacio who told me, "If, when we dance, our hearts are right, the rain will come." There were many memories as I watched the candles flicker at his side—memories of him and of the others who had preceded him. Just the month before, stooped and almost blind, he had served at the Mass for Tonita. He had lived a long and full and active life. The moccasins beneath his blanket were well worn. He would have been unhappy sitting by the fire. I miss him as I shall miss Juan Estevan and Sayah, but I cannot mourn.

Summer was dry and hot—so hot. I searched in vain for Mariposa lilies in June, though in May the hills had been gay with flowers. The weeks seemed an endless round of gathering vegetables and preparing meals. There was tension and accelerated activity on the Hill with the men "going south." Explosions on the Plateau seemed to increase and then to cease. Men were in the Pacific, leaving wives on the Hill. Things—unknown things, were happening.

The climax came on that August day when the report of the atomic bomb flashed around the world. It seemed fitting that it was Kitty Oppenheimer who, coming for vegetables, brought the news. I had not known what was being done up there, though in the beginning I had suspected atomic research. Much was now explained. Now I can tell you that Conant and Compton came in through the kitchen door to eat ragout and chocolate cake; that Fermi and Allison, Teller, Parsons, came many times; that Oppenheimer was the man I knew in pre-war years and who made it possible for the Hill people to come down; that Hungarians, Swiss, Germans, Italians, Austrians, French and English have been serious and gay around the candlelit table. It has been an incredible experience for a woman who chose to live in a supposedly isolated spot. In no other place could I have had the privilege of knowing Niels Bohr who is not only a great scientist but a great man. In no other way could I have seen develop a group feeling of responsibility for presenting the facts to the people and urging the only wise course—international control of atomic energy and the bomb.

Perhaps the desperate state of the world and the anguish of millions as the constant backdrop of life intensified the joys that fall always brings. This year there were trips to the Plateau for wood on days when sky and aspen vied with each other in beauty. The wind made melody in tall pines while I gathered pine knots. They seemed to be the essence of the elements garnered by a tree and now released in the fireplace to complete the cycle. Their gathering has become as much a part of the fall ceremonies as the garden harvesting and the southward flight of geese. The rhythmic order of nature holds for me assurance as well as beauty.

FOURTEEN

On THE SUMMER DAY when the newspapers of the world first spread the words "atomic bomb" in towering headlines, I remembered a dream I had the month before. I was alone in my house that night and slept restlessly. Around 2 A.M. I woke from my dream with a sense of deep foreboding. For some reason I did not understand I put on my robe and slippers and went outside into the still moonlight. It seemed a perfectly tranquil summer night. The sky was familiar with its clock of stars. The houses below my hill were silent; no dogs barked; only birds made sleepy noises. Yet I went back into the house with a weight of uneasiness on me and for the first time since I had lived in the Taos valley I locked all my doors. Still I could not go back to sleep. The dream haunted me and at last I sat up in bed with my pen and notebook and wrote it down. What I wrote was this:

"I was riding on a bus with my mother and my children. I held a carpet-sweeper in my hand. All at once a strange and overwhelming wind arose. We could see it coming down from the mountains and sweeping along the roads in the form of hundreds of small upward-spiralling whirlpools, like the twisters or dust-devils that are familiar in this region in spring and summer. The mouths of the whirling winds had a strong sucking action. The carpet-sweeper I was holding was wrenched from my hand. A group of Indians riding on horseback was pulled off the ground as they raced along the road.

"We stopped at a small mountain inn, and though the wind had quieted there were great broken branches in all the fields and twisted pieces of buildings that had been destroyed. I looked toward

the mountains and saw spiralling streamers of wind forming again and feared that in them was an irresistible, an invincible force that was about to destroy the earth. It was no ordinary wind but a great cosmic power unleashed that men could not deal with and that haunted me with its suggestion of doom."

When I looked back through my journal to see when I had dreamed this dream my skin grew cold. The date was July 16, only three hours before the first test explosion of the bomb at Alamogordo, the test so ironically labelled "Trinity." Even as I lay dreaming a little group of men from Los Alamos was shivering in the predawn chill of a semi-desert three hundred miles distant from our moonlit valley. They were watching for the signs of a dawn which for all they knew might be their last. None could be certain, in spite of all the careful calculations, of the exact effect of the power that was about to be unleashed. None knew for certain whether the doom of the world might not be about to issue from men's hands.

Reading Edith Warner's Christmas letter that year I was a little puzzled by her calm acceptance of those whom she now knew were responsible for the ruin of Hiroshima and Nagasaki. I could hardly bear to think that such destruction had been rooted in the heart of our once sacred world, that the man who put the bomb together just before it was dropped over Hiroshima had lived for awhile in my own house where the wisteria still flowered against the window and the apricot trees I had planted when my children were tiny had only just begun to bear their fruit. Whenever I went to the little house by the river I found myself pouring forth streams of condemnation against those who had usurped our places on the plateau, and I sometimes thought in Edith's and Tilano's hearts as well.

Edith's silence in the face of my disputes did more to untangle the knot of resentment in my heart than anything she said. The mesas were still there—"those ancient beings who have seen much"—and she let them speak. In time I was able to think of the men and women on the Hill as human beings whose hearts had been torn like mine by the world's pain, to understand how they must have found healing in the quiet of the little house, walking

where I had walked in the cool glade by the river where the cow switched her tail and stamped at flies, and the turkeys strutted and spread their snow-white fans.

Edith spoke very little of her new friends except now and then to tell me of the neighborly visits of the women who came down for eggs or vegetables or new-baked bread. Reticence was still very much part of her nature and the habit of secrecy that had grown on us all through the war years forbade me to ask questions. The conversations that took place in the adobe dining room will probably never be reported. She herself took almost no part in them. On the rare occasions when she could be persuaded to join the company after dinner she would listen, as she did when the wise men of the pueblo talked, saying nothing unless she were asked a persistent question. Then she would furrow her brow a little and make a remark as down to earth and simple as the bread she served. She always felt that she had no gift for words; she had strong opinions on many matters but it was hard to draw them out of her. Instead of the vague word she offered the thing itself, candlelight reflected from the glossy black surface of the pottery bowls, the smell of piñon wood that whispered as it burned in the corner fireplace, the walls of the house she had made so warm against the wind.

It is odd that almost no one remembers anything special Edith said.

"It is her smile I remember best," one man has told me. "A beautiful smile, not sad, and ever so slightly amused. What it signified was not exactly wisdom, and not any kind of stoic acceptance, perhaps just Acquaintance contrasted with knowledge-about—certainly one of the elements of wisdom." This is philosophical language and Edith would have laughed to think of it being applied to her. But there was some quality in her nature that made her quick to respond to the presence of true wisdom, whether it leapt into her recognition from a mesa, a riverworn stone, or the sensitive and seeking face of a human being. Whether the face was brown-skinned or white seemed to make no difference. Wisdom was of the gods, she always felt, and her greatest respect was given to those whose lives, like her own, remained humble toward the mystery of truth. I will

always remember the special light in her eyes when she mentioned the most improbable of all her acquaintances, the great Danish physicist, Niels Bohr.

How strangely fate moved to bring these two together. In the autumn of 1922 when Edith Warner had just begun to explore the trails of beauty in Frijoles Canyon, Bohr was awarded the Nobel prize for his research into the structure of the atom. During the nineteen-thirties, while Edith was living so quietly by the Rio Grande, pondering on the invisible energies that seemed to flow into her from sky and mesa, Niels Bohr, at his own Institute for Theoretical Physics at the University of Copenhagen, was wrestling with the great dualities that science had discovered in the minutest particles of matter and devising theories to reconcile their conflict. He is most widely known today for the theory or philosophy to which he has given the name "Complementarity," a word which is still unknown to most of us in its technical sense, but which has begun to affect deeply the way men think about the world—and about themselves. The theory arose out of what seemed mutually exclusive ways of regarding light as composed either of waves or of particles. Bohr helped to resolve the conflict by suggesting that wave and particle are really different aspects of the same thing. Everything depends on the standpoint of the observer, each point of view giving a partial image which excludes, but also supplements the other. "What the theory really means," says one interpreter, "is that harmony in nature consists of an interplay of apparently conflicting forces." This seems to me like a curious reflection of something that Edith Warner's pueblo neighbors have always known. The dual nature of life reveals itself to them in the relation between earth and sky, between summer and winter, between the male and female potencies in all that lives. They have no theories about such things. What they know is instinctive and expressed not in abstract words but in the patterns of design and ritual through which earth and sky are brought together.

The Hopi have a saying, quoted by Mary Austin in her *Land of Journeys Ending*, "Straight as the Sacred Meal road over which the gods pass into the images of themselves." Physicists would never name the powers they deal with "gods" but the best of them, and

certainly Niels Bohr is among these, have an attitude which can only be described as reverence toward the ceaseless transformations of energy that take place in the smallest elements of the physical world as well as in the seething nebulae in space.

Preoccupied as they were with the concern to find what the world is made of, it was only at the beginning of the second World War that the scientists of the world began to concern themselves seriously with the technical uses of atomic energy. Ironically it was Niels Bohr, with his great humanistic spirit, his ideal of scientific cooperation between men of every nation, who in 1939 came to America with the ominous news that the Germans were experimenting with nuclear fission and had succeeded in splitting an atom of uranium. As a result of this information the Manhattan Project came into being, which led to the establishment of the secret laboratories at Los Alamos.

For a time, Bohr returned to his own work in Denmark, but in 1943 he was warned that the Nazis were taking steps to arrest him. He and his wife managed to escape, first to neutral Sweden and then to London. In 1944 he was sent to the United States as a member of the British team which worked with the Manhattan Project. Under the wartime incognito of "Nicholas Baker" he made several visits to Los Alamos—and thus became part of the extraordinary legend of Edith Warner and the house at Otowi Bridge.

At Los Alamos, Bohr—whose standing in Denmark is said to be "only slightly less sacred than that of the royal family and Hans Christian Andersen"—was known to his friends as "Uncle Nick." He has been described as a large man, fond of athletics and all outdoor activity, who smoked a pipe and wore a big straw hat that made him look more like a fisherman than a physicist. "He is a soft-spoken, extremely gentle person," one physicist friend tells me, "very warm, friendly, unassuming. He is very difficult to understand in any language, because of his habit of mumbling and speaking in unfinished sentences and elliptical phrases, which suggest rather than communicate. Miss Warner was not much of a talker either, so their very real rapport must have come from more than conversation, from a mutual feeling of spiritual kinship, love of humanity and of nature."

I have seen a picture of Niels Bohr taken long after Edith knew him. He looks like a benevolent grandfather—as indeed he is—with thinning gray hair and shaggy eyebrows in a face as wide and round as though a child had drawn it. His expression reminds me of a snapshot I still have of one of my children, a very small boy he was then, intent and wondering as he probes with one finger the center of a flower he bends toward him. There seems to me a certain look of sadness, the sadness, perhaps, of a man who realizes the part he has played in putting into man's hands a terrible power for life and for destruction, and who has tried ever since to open the minds of statesmen to their responsibility for seeing that this power is controlled and used for the benefit of humanity and not its doom. In 1950 Niels Bohr addressed an open letter to the United Nations in which he said in part,

"An open world where each nation can assert itself solely to the extent to which it can contribute to the common culture and is able to help others with experience and resources must be the goal to be put before everything else. . . . The development of technology has now reached a stage where the facilities for communication have provided the means for making all mankind a cooperating unity . . . at the same time fatal consequences to civilization may ensue unless international divergences are considered as issues to be settled by consultation based on free access to all relevant information."

This great letter, with its prophetic warning, was set aside by the United Nations, for the statesmen of the world were not yet ready to learn new ways of dealing with one another. The copy of it which I have here is autographed by Niels Bohr "To Mrs. Benjamin Ludlow in gratitude for the friendship of your sister."

Edith Warner scarcely mentions this friendship in any of her letters. Her feeling for people was something deep within her, like her response to the mesas and the river. She sometimes spoke of Niels Bohr in connection with her "high places"—those mountain and mesa tops where earth and sky come closest to each other and exchange their substance. What she meant is made clearer to me in a letter from Mrs. Miller:

"I remember once saying to godmother, after I had been walking along Shumo, that the mesa struck me with a terrible familiarity in

every line, and I realized that something I knew very well in Tilano was there in the mesa. Her smile was that glowing one as she said, "Yes, of course—they are different forms of the same thing."

What she found in Niels Bohr was the "same thing" she saw in the mesas and in Tilano, as I think she is struggling to say in this paragraph from one of her letters to her goddaughter:

Nothing comes by leaps and bounds but by years. Eventually one should be able to make a "high place" within, but not for one's own use. I know now that if I never see "Mr. Baker" again, I have had the important thing he had to give me, the knowledge that what I thought beyond man's compass can be so strong in a human being that it radiates, and yet does not make him a "master."

What seems to have touched her especially was the humility of this great man who is said always to tell his students, "Every sentence I utter must be understood, not as an affirmative, but as a question," and of whom Einstein said, shortly before his death, "Personally Bohr is one of the most amiable colleagues I have ever met. He utters his opinions like one perpetually groping and never like one who believes himself to be in the possession of definite truth."

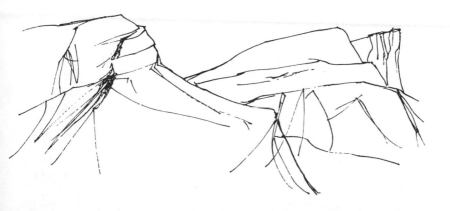

"Godmother always felt she had something to learn from him," Peter Miller writes me. "I remember her saying that she felt for a long time that he might give her a magic word. This was one of the last things she ever talked to me about—and then smiling she said, 'But now I know that there *is* no magic word or any need for any!' "

Who knows what Niels Bohr remembers as he romps with his grandchildren in faraway Denmark—the bright sun of New Mexico, the sudden shadows, the air scented after each rain with sagebrush and juniper? I like to think that Dr. Philip Morrison, one of the physicists who shared the long ago hours of seriousness and gaiety "around the candlelit table" was speaking for him as well as for many others when in 1945 he wrote this letter to Edith Warner:

"You will realize that we have all been changed by our years on the Mesa. We worked passionately for the great end we achieved, knowing that it was really no end but a means. In that work we changed. We had to learn again in all its meaning how strong is the bond between science and the life of men. We shall never forget our time on the Hill. The time was made of long night hours and of critical discussions, of busy desert days and patient waiting in the laboratory; it held the terrible suspense of the last minutes at Trinity. There was more. We lived in a community. We grew to know each other. But that was hardly novel; most of us had been friends long before Los Alamos. What was new was the life around us we began to share. We learned to watch the snow on the Sangres and to look for deer in Water canyon. We found that on the mesas and in the valley there was an old and strange culture; there were our neighbors, the people of the pueblos, and there were the caves in Otowi canyon to remind us that other men had sought water in this dry land. Not the smallest part of the life we came to lead, Miss Warner, was you. Evenings in your place by the river, by the table so neatly set, before the fireplace so carefully contrived, gave us a little of your assurance, allowed us to belong, took us from the green temporary houses and the bulldozed roads. We shall not forget.

"It was a terrible irony that brought the makers of bombs to the quiet Otowi crossing. It would have been easy for you to reject our problem. You could have drawn away from the Hill people and

their concerns and remained in the compact life of the valley. But you did not. We take from that the hope that people of intelligence and goodwill everywhere can understand and share our sense of crisis. In that hope lies the world's best assurance. I am glad that at the foot of our canyons there is a house where the spirit of Bohr is so well understood."

Almost fourteen years later when I wrote Dr. Morrison for permission to use his letter he summed up his feeling in these words:

"Miss Warner, her home by the river, and her spirit of grace remain a part of everyone at Los Alamos lucky enough to have known her . . . Edith Warner stands in the history of those desperate times as a kind of rainbow . . . a sign that war and bombs are not all that men and women are capable of building."

FIFTEEN

AFTER THE WAR, atomic research continued and the city of Los Alamos kept on growing till it was a blaze of light under the night sky, and the old bridge across the Rio Grande was no longer adequate for the increasing flow of traffic. Supplies and building materials for the city, and heavy equipment for the laboratories, were brought in by motor truck. The narrow-gauge railway had been abandoned, its tracks pulled up. Workers by the hundreds from the pueblos and the Spanish-American villages along the river and from as far away as Santa Fe commuted daily. By Christmas of 1946, Edith Warner learned that the plans for the new bridge would bring the world into her dooryard, almost beneath her kitchen window. With the constant roar of heavy trucks her cherished peace and seclusion would no longer be possible. Life in the little house would not even be endurable. There was nothing to do but move.

Tilano at first refused to leave. He was around eighty now, and set on living out his years at the place-where-the-river-makes-a-noise. How can a man, when he is old, tear out his roots from the soil made of the fallen leaves of his long years? Edith was fifty-four, unaware that she had only five more years of life. Her one concern was to find a place where Tilano could live out his years happily. "Without him" she said, "the twenty years at the bridge would have been impossible." He had become her companion and helpmate, and the living bond with the earth into which her roots had gone so deep. "For many the little house at the river was a landmark, for some an experience. For me it was two decades of living and learning," Edith said in her letter of 1947.

With the instinct of a bird to rebuild its nest, a spider to re-spin the torn web, she kept on searching until she found a place that would suit Tilano. It was about half a mile away, up the canyon and opposite the garden on the other side of the arroyo which enters the Rio Grande just south of the bridge. The site was withdrawn, secluded, screened from the highway by spice bushes and juniper and a tall grove of cottonwood. The river could be heard only on occasional very still days. They would no longer be able to see the Black Mesa which had seemed the immovable point around which the tides of color in the valley shifted. Instead the arm of To-tavi came close around them, the tawny-rose slope of river gravel capped by a miniature palisade of black basaltic rock. Over the bare shoulder of the mesa a trail led upward into the world of bare rock and secret hidden springs. The animal world seemed closer than the world of humans.

Tilano agreed that the place had possibilities. The land belonged to the pueblo; in the slow Indian way it took four months for the council to decide that a house could be built here. These were months of tension, of heartache, and again the repeated discipline of patience. Over and over Edith found herself facing what reason said was impossible. And over and over solutions came in the most unexpected manner, and at last a demonstration of friendship and love that seemed like a miracle.

Looking back to those dry windy days when I was faced with building a house and a road, finding water, moving stable, corral and chicken houses, I am certain it was a miracle. I had only a few hundred dollars and some old lumber. But Tilano and I had friends, more than we knew. There were those who had found in the guest house rest for weary bodies and minds; those who had watched the morning light move across the mesas and been renewed.

No one knows who first thought of building the new house for Edith. The thought seemed to start spontaneously in many minds. Some gave interest and advice; some offered financial assistance; there were others, and they came from both sides of the river, from the centuries-old pueblo, and from the new city on the mesa, who

gave unstintingly of the strength of their hands and their hours of leisure.

In May of 1947, Tony Pena from the pueblo started to make adobe bricks in the garden, bricks out of earth where corn had grown the year before, earth and water and straw mixed together, shaped in wooden forms, dried in the brilliant sunlight to enduring hardness. Tilano had decided the exact spot where the house would stand and had marked the outline of the foundations. On the last week end in the month Facundo and Sandy, Tony and Juanita came over from San Ildefonso in their wagons. There was no road yet; everything must be hauled across the sandy arroyo that often ran with unpredictable water. The foundations of the house—long trenches filled with stones—were laid out in the rain. Tony and Tilano looked happy and said it was good. The rain was an assurance that prayers were potent, that the hearts of the builders were right.

About fifteen people from Los Alamos had asked to help, young physicists with their wives, men who had participated in the birth of the atomic bomb, women who had shared the long months of tension before the test explosion. Now they began to work side by side with the men and women from San Ildefonso. The men hauled rocks in the creaking wagons; women fitted them into the trenches and mixed mud. Children played in the arroyo where Tilano had dug holes for them in the sand and uncovered hidden water.

This was a good day; it was the beginning of many days that had in them all the quality an Indian thinks of when he says that rain

is "good" or that a man's heart is "good." They were days of hard work, week end after week end in the hot summer sun, exhausting physical effort, unaccustomed muscles that had to be held under the discipline of mind and will till they learned the function which to the pueblo men and women came as naturally as breathing. Pine saplings had to be peeled with backbreaking motions and aching, blistered hands. There were floors to be laid, one of brick, the others of adobe; there were oceans of mud to be mixed and carried for plastering.

Tilano and Tony bossed the physicists. Frustrated scientists sometimes suggested more efficient methods, but efficiency never became much of a consideration. The Indians had a know-how that was built into the fibers of their nerves and muscles. "This is the way we do it," they would say, always without hesitation, the eye noting more accurately than any measure whenever an angle was out of line, whenever a curve had become unbalanced. Women down on their hands and knees smoothing a floor would smile and try again, when Tilano with a grandfatherly tolerance would say, "No, not *that* way, *this* way."

"Sometimes we felt that during the week the Indians would undo our work and do it over again," one scientist said ruefully, learned as he was in all the intricacies of atomic motion.

Walls rose with amazing speed. No Ph.D. or his wife was ever allowed to set one brick on another; they carried the adobes and handed them, obedient as children helping father, to Tony who laid each carefully in its place. Over the walls the vigas were lifted and rested, old beams from the pueblo, new straight logs from the forests above Truchas and beyond Puyé. On top of the vigas the peeled pine saplings were laid. These were covered with roofing paper and mud and more paper, then tar, and then more dirt, a good roof, upheld by the good hearts of those who had helped build it.

"When it was time to cover the walls with plaster, first rough, then smooth," Edith told us, "the Pueblo people sent word they wanted to do it. The men mixed the mud and carried it to the women. Some kneaded it and handed it to those who with skilled hands covered the adobe bricks. There was much talk and laughter and always a beautiful rainbow motion of the hand."

At lunch every one relaxed under the cottonwoods in the meadow. A simple meal was served—ragout, homemade bread, garden lettuce, big slabs of chocolate cake. Tilano leaned against an old tree. His face was lined, but these were lines made by a lifetime of wind and sunlight, of laughter and tenderness. It was a happy face, as though the winds that had touched his life had all been gentle ones. He seemed like the tree he leaned against, whose leaves move in the slightest wind, but whose roots hold firmly. The letter of 1947 warmed all our hearts with this gentle picture:

When Tilano lights the little fire on Christmas Eve, those to whom it pays respect will know that human beings now live where last winter only quail, rabbits and coyote made patterns in the snow.

SIXTEEN

THE FIRST WINTER in the new house was a hard one. Edith could not help being homesick at first for the little house that had meant for her "two decades of living and learning." In her next letter she writes:

The blue heron has not followed us from the river to the side of To-tavi-kadi, mesa of the quail. I miss hearing him as he flew homeward after his late supper; miss seeing him standing on one leg in the lagoon as he waited for a minnow to swim across his image here on a still night. . . .

In January a succession of storms piled snow on snow. The snow and the wood kept us busy. Each trip to the woodpile or the chicken yard was into a world where white mesas glistened against a deep blue sky, where snow-covered trees shook starry flakes from their branches. From the wide window near the fireplace we saw storm clouds gather over the mountains, or sunset turn the peaks bright red.

It was the winter that Donicio died, he who had been the center in a line of dancers. The chorus grouped itself around him for the Corn Dance; the song seemed to come from him. The feeling of loss weighed upon Edith's heart, though she knew that soon the dance would group itself around another center.

The house still seemed very new. It had not yet begun to blend with the earth from which it had been made, yet already when the first geese flew south they had discovered it. They flew north again early in February. Her new life began to be woven once more into the rhythm of the seasons. The stormy winter had brought a wealth

of blossom to the stony hillside. By the well she watched a bud unfold upon a slender stalk, wondering if she had dreamed the exquisite cream-colored Mariposa lily, three-petalled, with its center of bright gold. She had seen them bloom before only on the high mesa west of the river. How patiently the seeds must have waited through the long dry years for the moisture to waken them.

Summer brought guests again. The garden yielded its abundance. On the new window ledge the pots of mint and chives grew green among the scarlet blossoms of geranium. Children came down to play under the cottonwoods in the arroyo bottom. Old Los Alamos boys brought wives and babies for a taste of chocolate cake. Scientists left for far parts of the world, hoping someday to return. "This is a changing world," Edith wrote us. "Perhaps what they really want is to find the essence unchanged. This becomes my challenge."

In September she made a feast for the pueblo. About a hundred came in cars and wagons to see the new house and to have dinner. This too was a link between the old life and the new. In the first days of the adobe guest house, the whole village had come over one evening for a housewarming. The children had been put to sleep after supper in the small bedroom. In the living room they had danced to the sound of the drum and Indian voices singing. At the end of the dance one of the men had put a turquoise necklace around Edith's neck; María presented her with a small carved wooden santo.

In the ten years since the guest-house party, much had changed. Many of the Pueblo boys who danced that other evening had been to war, some in France, some in England, some in the Pacific. Now they were back in their own sacred world, but never again would the mountains of the four directions be the limits of that world. The war was over but peace had not yet been secured. "The scientists know that they cannot go back to their laboratories leaving atomic energy in the hands of the armed forces and the statesmen," Edith wrote us. "Nor can I concern myself only with my kitchen, for I too am one of the people."

Once someone asked her if it were true that the Pueblos had developed a way of life that protected them from the frustrations and

tensions which the white world seemed to be facing. She smiled. "These people are human beings like ourselves," she told him, "with their own full share of human good and ill."

She resisted the temptation that many white people feel to idealize the Indians, the effort to find in this ancient culture all that seems lacking in our own. In the same way she realized how the younger Indians, resisting the bondage of their own tradition, look to the white man's way as an escape. How well she understood that neither way can be completely fulfilled without the other. The two forms of knowledge, the two patterns of living, must somehow fertilize each other so that the gods may live their great polarities in human hearts as well as in all nature. The knowledge that leads to power, and the wisdom that grows from the service of the earth and the love of its beauty existed side by side for her, as though they were the opposite banks between which the great river flowed.

After this last "feast" Edith decided that it was more satisfactory to invite her Indian neighbors to visit her a family at a time. Tomacita and Facundo who had danced as Buffalo three years before, celebrated their tenth wedding anniversary with her. The small son, Nahn-tu, who had slept in his cradle in the ceremonial house during the dance, now shared his place with a long-lashed baby sister. Teen, who at two had watched the dance with Edith, was now a schoolboy.

In the fall there were trips to the mesa for wood and to gather pine knots, "those multi-shaped legacies of forgotten trees." Many of the old roads were fenced, but Navawi'i, where John Boyd had first showed her the hollowed deer pit, was still accessible. In the midst of the plateau now dominated by Los Alamos the Government had set aside a "sacred area" where the San Ildefonso people were still allowed to tend their ancient shrines and perform the ceremonies that insured the earth's fertility. Aspen still flamed in gold up the sides of the Jemez Mountains. Turkey still called in the deep canyons, and the sunlight was warm and mixed with the scent of dried grass and juniper. Near a tumbled ruin she found a trail worn deep in the rock and a woman's thumb print still visible on a sherd of her pottery.

"There alone in the sunlight," she said, "I began to understand that nothing men may do, not even the atomic bomb, can in anyway touch or change the essence of this country."

SEVENTEEN

TWO YEARS of sun and snow weathered the new house and rooted it deeply in the side of the sheltering mesa. Slowly Edith began to feel the new spirit grow. The design became clear again, as though a new fabric were being woven from the raveled strands of the old. While Edith had wanted the house in the beginning especially for Tilano, it seemed essential that it have meaning for others.

How was it possible to develop quickly that which at the old house had grown slowly and unplanned over a long period of years? How could it be shared when no commercial reason drew people? For these problems there was no established method. It was not a picture to be painted, a poem to be written. It was not even mine to create. So I lived each day as it presented itself and hoped I would find the way. . . . Perhaps I can make you see now how the growing spirit of this house is compounded of the earth itself and the seasons, of daily living, and in great measure of the people who come to it.

When I go to feed the chickens each morning my eyes make the circle of the compass, beginning with the basaltic point of To-tavi in the west. Memory supplies its long line above the river, the quiet place on its side where I go to be alone, a tiny crescent ruin covered with dry grasses that shine in the sun, and across the river, the carved face of Shumo whose northern point is visible. Beyond the valley rise the mountains with Lake Peak sharply outlined against the sky, and in the north T'omo, like a great outstretched prehistoric creature above the road to Los Alamos. These deeply rooted steadfast

mesas provide a bulwark for living in this age, and at the same time present beauty ever changing in color and aspect. On their sides and high places are ceremonial trails and shrines where for centuries men have placed prayer plumes when their hearts were right. Closer and more intimate is the hillside with its old trail, where I have found stones carried long ago in a buckskin pouch. From it the quail come down near the house, and a rabbit nibbles the grass unafraid. Above it the crescent winter moon shines, and this month Venus is the evening star.

I am glad the first winter was one of storm and cold because it necessitated spending many more hours indoors. Tilano's room, with its fireplace and sunlight on clear days quickly becomes the lived-in center of the house. Here hang his dance costume—buckskin leggings, fox-skin, bells, and the pictures of the children who call him uncle. Here feathers are sorted and tied with care for the dancers; a headdress or bow and arrows are made for some child; and from his chair he watches in unceasing wonder the cars going to and from Los Alamos. Sometimes there are guests for tea, as color follows color from foothills to sky. Sometimes on winter evenings there are tales of long ago. From here he went, when it was time to prepare for the Buffalo dance, to the pueblo, and returned with the quality of those days spent apart still on him.

I wish you might see the big kitchen on some Sundays, on Thanksgiving, during Christmas week, on many a day throughout the years. Sometimes it is little blond children, sometimes black-haired children who run into the kitchen for a drink of water or a basket of toys. . . . A car may come from Santa Fe, or from the Hill, or across the valley with someone who needs to sit awhile here and look at the mountains or the hillside. Rosanita came to celebrate her graduation as a nurse, Louis and Juanita their wedding anniversary. Hagi, who used to help in the garden as a little boy, and who hauled all the water for the house-building, came with his parents after graduation to discuss his future. Several months later he returned in a Marine uniform to "tell us all about it." Peter and Earle bring weeks of merriment and talk. All year our friends and friends of theirs drive across the arroyo to see how we fare, to look at the mountains, to add a bit of themselves to the spirit of the house.

Nineteen-fifty was a year of drought and heartbreak. Edith told us how she napped in the sun on January twenty-third, the day of San Ildefonso's winter feast when one usually huddles to watch the ceremony wrapped in blankets. On Easter Day the wind blew stinging sand on the naked bodies and the horned heads of the Buffalo dancers. Fruit blossoms blackened with frost in May. Water flowed in a thin discouraging trickle in the irrigation ditches. In June the corn and beans dried under a cloudless sky. In July thunderstorms, brief and violent, washed out the road and filled the garden with gravel. Late in September a hailstorm washed the mud plaster off the housewalls. After that no rain fell at all. Late carrots had to be dug from the ground with a pick.

Edith found herself thinking often of the prehistoric people who centuries ago, after long drought, had abandoned their pueblos to the slow work of ruin while they journeyed to the south in hope of greener fields. They too must have scanned the sky with dwindling hope and finally with despair before they decided to leave their homes and sacred places, wondering if their ceremonies had lost the power to bring the rain.

Now on the high plateau where lizards scuttled among the bushes that grew thick in the roofless kivas, mankind was experimenting with another kind of power. It had been so far a power of death rather than of life. She thought of the thousands of homeless at Hiroshima and Nagasaki. How strange it seemed that the bomb which had created such waste and such suffering had been made on the plateau where the ancient people for so long invoked their gods in beauty. In the smallest atoms of dust the forces that hold the worlds together lay slumbering. Long ago men had learned to call them forth with prayer, with the prayer of dancing bodies, of soaring voices, making themselves one with the need of earth for rain. "If our hearts are right the rain will come," Ignacio had said. Had men forgotten the wisdom of the heart, the knowledge that all men everywhere are of one substance?

She remembered how the candlelight had shone upon the sensitive faces of the scientists in the little house by the river. How gaily these men had talked of their children, of mountain climbing and of music. It was hard to believe they had been working day and

night to split the atom and release its energy for the use of man, the violent use of man. In the days after Hiroshima she had seen many of these men recoil at the implications of what they had done. She had seen the realization grow among them that now irrevocably the world was one. As the community of knowledge had led to the discovery of atomic fission so now it must lead men to deal with the great power that had been unleashed. There were no frontiers left, behind which one could live blindly.

"We know," Robert Oppenheimer has said, "how little of the deep new knowledge which has altered the face of the world, which has changed—and increasingly and ever more profoundly must change—man's views of the world, resulted from the quest for practical ends or an interest in exercising the power that knowledge gives. For most of us, in most of those moments when we were most free of corruption, it has been the beauty of the world of nature and the strange and compelling harmony of its order, that has sustained, inspirited, and led us."

The beauty of the world of nature—in spite of all the threat and hardship that was woven into life she could not doubt it. The energy in the atom—was it really different from that which slept in the waiting seed, in the sunlight released from blazing pine knots, in the stone that pulsed under the fingers that touched it rightly, in the hearts of those who worked together to rebuild what had been destroyed?

How to endure the man-made devastating period in which we live and which seems almost hopeless to control as drought; how to proceed when leadership seems utterly lacking, when individuals and nations seem stupid and arrogant; these are questions no human can answer. I only know that the power recognized by those other sky-scanners still exists, that contact is possible. I know, too, what depths of kindness and selflessness still exist in my fellow-men. . . . When Tilano lights the Christmas Eve fire, perhaps against a white hillside, I shall watch from the house where some have felt peace, and hope that in your sky are some bright stars.

EIGHTEEN

During one of her early days at the bridge, Edith wrote this paragraph in her journal:

On gray days like this I often think of the wild geese flying south. I heard their honking one October day and went out into the gently falling rain to see the swaying black line of them against the gray sky. Soon they entered the canyon and I watched them closely, following against the dark mesa the darker line. Now above, now below the broken mesa rim they flew with never a moment of hesitation, with always the memory of warm, plentiful feeding grounds, and an old trail leading to them. Where the river turns again, they rose above the mesa, and my last glimpse of them was that swaying line against the lighter clouds, winging southward. Death could be like that.

It was late in November of 1950. We were involved in war again. This time in Korea. I and my son, who was soon to enter the Army, drove down from Taos to spend a last afternoon with Edith and Tilano. It was a day as beautiful and warm as summer. We sat in the sunshine outside the kitchen door in the crisp scent of juniper, talking lightly and throwing sticks for the little dog to fetch. Tilano told us of the fox he had seen run down the mesa point only a little above the house, and of the deer tracks in the bushes near the garden. Age sits lightly on the men of the Pueblos and it was hard to realize that he was nearly eighty. His long hair in its braids was as black as ever. His eyes were still bright as a bird's. The child and the wise old man were balanced in him.

Edith seemed frail; some digestive trouble had been plaguing her, but she laid it to the strenuous year, the constant anxiety over the strange weather, the struggles with the garden. "Rest and diet are bound to bring me back to normal and mesa-climbing soon," she told us smiling. She was fifty-eight that year. Her thin hair was quite white, and her eyes behind the wide-rimmed glasses were the untroubled color of spring water. How could I ever have thought her a nonentity, I wondered, remembering that early summer when she had wandered in from the forest above Anchor Ranch with her hands full of wildflowers and I had pigeonholed her as just another sentimental tenderfoot?

Now I was the mother of three grownup sons. My youngest—the boy who had wept over the closing of Los Alamos—was recovering from polio. My eldest son was married and I had a grandson. The second boy, whose feet Tilano is washing in the childhood picture, was a young man sitting here beside me. Edith was giving him her woman's blessing as she had given it to so many brown-skinned Pueblo boys whose time had come to go to far-off wars. She gave it wordlessly as always, the cup of tea, the slice of chocolate cake, the peace and quietness of the autumn afternoon. Little did I dream in that moment that all three of my sons would find their lifework in fields connected with atomic energy. The eldest was already an electronics engineer; his brother was to follow him. The youngest went safely enough I thought, into meteorology, but he, too, has taken part in atomic tests in Nevada and at Eniwetok. I suppose no generation has grown up to live in a world so changed from that of their own childhood. Los Alamos has become a city of thirteen thousand and our life on the mesa seems like a chapter in ancient history.

As usual that afternoon I complained to Edith about the complexities of my life and as usual she was all gentle sympathy. I was still bitter at having been exiled from the plateau. The roots of my childhood and of my young womanhood were deep there. I never drove past the forbidding fences without tears in my eyes, and my hatred of the new city of Los Alamos was still sore. I had not learned, even from Edith, that out of the death of the old, life is continually being reborn. I had not yet realized that the gods of

cloud and mountain move within us, or that the center of the sacred world is in ourselves.

Edith surprised me that afternoon by speaking eagerly of a power-line that might soon be built near enough to the house that she could have electricity. She too, I thought resentfully, was willing to abandon the past, the magic of the simple life that had been hers, for the doubtful blessing of "modern conveniences."

"Tilano is too old to keep hauling water from the well," she told me. "If we could have a pump he could live out his days in peace." I knew then that it was no longer possible to go on dreaming that one could live in a house by the side of the road and not be part of the changing life that goes on flowing past it.

In January of 1951 I learned with dismay that Edith had gone to Chicago to have an operation. When the surgeons found they could do nothing for her, they allowed her to return home. They did not tell her that the situation was hopeless, but I am sure she knew. We who loved her fought against the knowledge as long as we could. She had been home only a week when her condition became suddenly critical. More for our sakes than her own, and most especially because of Tilano, she allowed herself to be taken to the very modern hospital at Los Alamos. There was a new treatment with radioactive gold which some dared hope might cure her. For a few weeks she seemed to be getting better, and we held our breaths. It would have seemed like the greatest of miracles if Los Alamos which had given us the bomb could also have given us her life. But in March a letter came from her neighbor, Ethel Froman:

"Edith is at home and has decided to try nothing more. . . . Intellectually she is right, perhaps, but it is hard to understand. . . . We felt Edith just couldn't give up. . . . I guess the cancer

is so widespread that no one could hold out hope of any treatment doing any real good, and she is unwilling to go through any more just to be kept alive. Do write to her. She has told me how words as you can use them mean so much to her. . . . She is wonderful so far, worrying about my daughter Kay's stubbornly fixed baby, and Grandpa, and having Tilano give me their supply of milk-filters. Makes you wonder if you'd have strength yourself to be so calm, or would you just give way to hysterics? She's a wonderful person."

I was sure that for Edith it wasn't giving up, only an acknowledgment of where the trail was leading, and the determination to follow it, as the wild geese that rise at their autumn summons. In her fifth year by the river she had written in her journal:

When I had a tooth extracted a few days ago I was very calm. As I sat in the chair I saw inwardly my mesas. From thought of them strength and calm seemed to come to me. I became tense at times, but as I thought of the mesas I relaxed. It was not that the fear ceased to exist, and then the pain, but that another thought was greater than me. That must explain what my Indian friend once said. She had felt a fear once that I did, but she said, "I am strong in my heart." Surely that is better than saying there is no fear, no pain.

It was the end of March when she went home for the last time; it was the time of wind and blowing dust, days like those when Chai used to cross the bridge to sit with her when she was alone by the river. She went home to the embrace of the mesas, to Tilano's gentle and unperturbed companionship, his strength and his belief in life's goodness that never faltered. A practical nurse was found to take care of her, a woman with quiet and capable ways, a little like an old-time mountain midwife. Her sister and her goddaughter came to be with her. I drove down to sit with them one afternoon when Edith was sleeping. The spring sunshine was warm around us. The sky was very blue. A few clouds made purple shadows on the mesas. The tips of the cottonwood leaves were beginning to unfold from the tight sheaths of their winter buds. I felt as though we were

waiting for a birth as much as for a death, as though the passage from life were not after all so different from the passage into it, as though Edith's spirit were only in labor to be free, like a child that must be delivered from its mother. Why have men made such an enemy of death, I began to wonder? Edith was wiser, who saw it only as a transition and went her way without struggle.

She made herself ready as though she were going on a journey. Books she had borrowed she made sure would be returned. Small items of daily life, like the milk filters she no longer would be needing, she passed on to others. From the mail-order catalogue she selected a two-year supply of blue jeans for Tilano, as though she realized just how much time there would be before he followed her. Knowing there would not be another Christmas she wrote us a last letter:

After weeks in a hospital it is especially wonderful to be here in Tilano's room. Here he can rub my arm to relax me and give me of his calm and strength. From the bed I can see the first light on the mountains, watch the snow clouds rise from the glistening Truchas peaks, follow the sunset color from the valley to the sky. I can feel the mesas even though I do not see them. It is a good place in which to wait for the passing from a rich, full life into whatever work lies beyond. Since I cannot be well to take care of Tilano, I am happy and at peace. I would have you think of me that way.

When I saw her last the flame of her life shone from her eyes like a candle lighted against the darkness of a window. On a buckskin thong at her throat she was wearing her talisman, a small river pebble, smooth and polished and yellow as old ivory. It seemed to me that everything superfluous had been stripped from her and that at the four corners of the sacred world the gods stood waiting. She died on the fourth of May in 1951, in the opening of the young leaves, when the Mariposa lilies on the mesa begin to push the dark weight of earth aside and reach toward the sunlight.

During one of those last weeks I dreamed that I went again to Edith's house. There were crowds of people tiring her with their

chatter. Then, in my dream, I saw the Indians, I saw Tilano's people, coming out of the pueblo fully costumed for the Buffalo Dance, dark-skinned against the pale desert background, bearing in their hands green boughs, symbols of undying life. It wasn't the season for the Buffalo Dance; in my dream I knew this. They were doing it especially for Edith. They were dancing to impart energy to the earth upon which she dwelt, to make it holy for her. And in my dream I knew that I must go away and leave her to them.

APPENDIX

EDITH WARNER'S CHOCOLATE LOAF CAKE

  2 eggs beaten
  1 cup granulated sugar
  2⅓ cups flour sifted three times
  ½ teaspoon salt
  2 level teaspoons baking powder
  1 teaspoon vanilla
  ½ cup milk

Mix eggs, sugar and flour, add milk gradually, add salt, vanilla and baking powder. Melt together 2 squares Bakers chocolate and ⅛ pound butter. Add melted ingredients and beat until light.

Icing

  3 heaping tablespoons cocoa
  1½ cups powdered sugar
  ½ teaspoon vanilla
  2 slices butter melted
    Enough coffee or milk to make the proper consistency.
    Sift sugar and cocoa. Mix and beat.

(High altitude experiment stations recommend reducing baking powder for each two cups of flour approximately ¼ to ½ tsp. for every rise in altitude of 2500 feet. Reducing the sugar and increasing the liquid as altitude increases may also improve the cake. In my own experiments I used cake flour sifted before measuring: 2½ cups flour and 2 level teaspoons double acting baking powder at sea level; 2⅓ cups flour and 1½ teaspoons baking powder at 5000 feet, 2⅓ cups flour plus one tablespoon and 1 teaspoon baking powder at 7000 feet. The cake has a tendency to be a little dry. Increase the milk at least a tablespoon at 5000 feet and two tablespoons at 7000 feet. I had the best result baking it in a 10-by-6-by-2-inch pan for about 40 minutes at 350° F. Be careful not to overbake. Take it out the minute a broom straw comes out clean! P.P.C.)

THE WOMAN WHO DWELLS

The woman who dwells at the place of healing by the river
sits singing and sings the shape of the gods from the four directions;
sings onto the horizon the four mountains where the gods dwell;
sings into the bare sky the small cloud moving in brightness;
sings into the bare earth the growing tip of the green corn;
sings the river into a singing curve around her;
sings herself into the center of herself, alive and listening.

The woman who dwells at the place of healing by the river
stirs not from her place, goes not to the far mountains,
soars not into the high sky, enters not the deep earth;
sings as she draws in the sand the circle of healing;
sings the gods from the four directions into that circle;
sings the growing cloud into the reach of her own heart;
sings herself into the spear of the green corn growing.

—Peggy Pond Church
April 1939

FOR TILANO OF SAN ILDEFONSO

There was a world died with your death, Tilano,
the world of your memories, the world of your ripened wisdom,
the world that revolved round your heart as our own earth around
    its axis.
Do you remember?
But time for you is memory no longer.
There is nothing to be recalled; there is no separation
from time past and time not yet come. You live in my thought still
where the eye of imagination once felt inward
into your hidden life. I sit beside you
saying no word, but feeling the life within you
as one feels the life of a mountain, a tree,
the sky with its first stars shining.
Your face so ancient and wise ripples too with laughter.
Your hands are gentle and strong, but the axe no longer
splits summer from the tree; the cow no longer
strays under the cottonwoods beside the river.
The fox runs free. The proud deer will be taken
by men with no prayer in their hearts.

Times have changed, Tilano,
had changed even while you lived. Wisdom died with you
that our times sorely need. How shall we learn your language,
a Bible written in rocks, in the rhythm of the seasons,
the miracle in the seed, in the branch of the fir tree,
the voice in a shell, in a bone, in a prayer plume planted
where invisible beings move? How shall we see God
in the stone, in the stream, in the jagged spear of the lightning,
in the deer we have killed, in the lion, in the eagle soaring?
How shall we ask of all things, as we must, forgiveness,
or humble ourselves before this life that fills us?

—Peggy Pond Church

I. Christmas 1943

MUSIC—the song of the Rio Grande and the canyon wren.
DIRECTOR—Fate.
NARRATOR—a fearsome woman, whose roots have been shaken but
     still are deep in the soil of New Mexico.

A year ago doubts assailed me. Could I swing this business with
gas rationed? Ought I put aside selfish desire and go back to the
outside world and a war job? I had not learned, in spite of much
experience, that I am not, and never have been, the guiding hand
in my life. Something—what I do not venture to say—has prevented
what I thought I wanted to do and pushed me into what I eventually
did. Also, no matter how uncertain the immediate future—or marginless—a solution has always presented itself in time. But so powerful were those doubts that I had unaccustomed colds and many
headaches during the winter. I finally decided to wait and see,
having hoarded sufficient for some months. I hope I have learned
at long last, for again the unforeseen has happened.

Into this fairly remote section last December came the Army,
commandeering Los Alamos School, Anchor Ranch and the small
native ranches on all the Pajarito Plateau for some very secret project. The construction company had just completed the building.
A new road is almost finished. Many civilians live there and the
whole area is guarded by soldiers. Santa Fe calls it a submarine base
—as good a guess as any! It leaves only Mrs. Frey at Frijoles and
me here at the river—and we are newcomers, comparatively speaking. After about thirty years Los Alamos was dissolved by a stroke

of Mr. Stimson's pen-evil magic. Workmen and material began to go by in great quantity so that the valley was quiet no longer. For a year it has continued.

Early in January I was asked on the spur of the moment—yes, a woman is the head—to help in the Indian Service work at San Ildefonso. So I worked on rationing, seed orders, canning, for a small sum until August. It was good to go to the Pueblo and see the people, and I enjoyed it. There are thirteen boys in the armed services and they needed letters. The bill in Congress, threatening the Pueblos, meant more letters.

Tilano and I began planting the garden in warm March days, fearfully—and late in April the unsuspecting fruit blossoms were frozen. However, vegetables survived and produced bountifully and profitably, being sent to Los Alamos all summer. It was good to work in the soil. The garden, where Tilano's father worked, has a special quality as well as its own charm. Even the bears came down to it this fall!

Along about April the X's began coming down from Los Alamos for dinner once a week, and they were followed by others. Stranger even than the Army's choosing this locality was that the civilian head should be a man I knew. He had stopped years ago on a pack trip, come back for chocolate cake, brought a wife, and now was to be my neighbor for the duration. So once again a woman talked women's talk in my kitchen, a child played with Tavi, the dog, and hunted white turkey feathers.

That beginning has increased until there are one or two groups on most nights for dinner. They come in through the kitchen door, talk a bit before leaving, and are booked up weeks ahead. Because they are isolated and need even this change for morale, I feel it is definitely a war job for me. In addition they are mostly interesting and so solve my need for people, though that seems well supplied. There is always someone—the trailer woman coming for milk and eggs, the road camp woman for milk, and both for talk with a woman.

Summer was hot and dry. Dust covered everything; grasshoppers ate Pueblo crops; dump trucks hauled gravel from the riverbed through the yard; surveyors drove stakes all over; drillers brought

an infernal machine into the yard to find what foundation the earth offered for a bridge; noise ceased only with nightfall. Fear lived with me—and then suddenly in the fall was lifted. The bridge is not to be built now—lack of material. The road via Española is being repaired. It would have taken part of the yard, perhaps the well house, and the only possible solution for life here seemed a high wall. That would mean that when I stand at the kitchen door, as I so often do for a moment, to look at the mesas, at the cotton-woods' new green or the chamisa golden in the fall, I'd be looking at a wall. Now those moments at the door have deeper meaning. Peter came in September with a friend. Fortunately there had been no house guests before, for the San Ildefonso women are working at Los Alamos daily and I've had no help. Fall was especially beautiful and I wangled enough free hours to climb mesas and enough gas to go up to Navawii for a picnic. All that and the kitchen gabfests compensated for the summer.

Winter means better radio reception, some time to read, walks for mail. I hope there will be snow. I have joined Foreign Policy Association and am reading West and Adamic on Jugoslavia. I still care intensely what happens in the world and wish I required less sleep so I might read more. Tilano has had rheumatism but is better and has discarded his cane. He helps me serve, which satisfies his need and real love of people. Julian's death was hard on him, but he enjoys Juanita's fine boy and Santana's new baby, the children home from school, the soldiers on furlough.

Soon it will be Christmas Eve and Tilano will light the little pitch-wood fire out near the well house to welcome those spirits that draw near on that night. Inside, candles will burn and juniper fragrance will fill the house. Then I shall think of you all and wish that I might share with you the beauty and the peace. The essence of this land fills me at such times—as whenever I give it opportunity—and I know that I have been given more than one human's share of joy.

II. Christmas 1944

Again I look back across the months to bring you a glimpse of their pattern here by the river. After the confusion and the fears of 1943, this year's peace and beauty stand out like shining peaks. I wish the world might have them too.

My wish for snow was fulfilled beyond my expectation and the Christmas Eve fire was encircled by fresh white snow. Only the oldest men in the Pueblo remember so much snow on the ground for so many weeks. Temperatures fell to 16 below zero some mornings, bringing thick fog to the valley. There was hoarfrost on every tiny weed stalk and juniper berry and the rising sun made a magic world for me to go out into for wood and water. I managed to keep the house warm and, with chains, to drive to the Pueblo when necessary. Mostly I walked for mail, breaking the trail after each new snow and enjoying it. It was wonderful to look out at the mesas and see them all white, especially after the very dry preceding winter. It meant grass for cattle, water in the ditches for irrigation, a continued life cycle for seeds waiting underground through dry years. Bad roads were something to be endured and forgotten.

The Los Alamosers, who had skiing until May, came all through the winter five nights a week for dinner until my arm rebelled. So after several weeks' rest, I reduced the weekly average to three nights, which I have maintained. With the increased population "on the hill" I could serve every night and still have a waiting list. My contact with them is necessarily casual but interesting and there are some I should like to know better. How long they will be there is secret as what they are doing. Building seems to continue, though I am scarcely conscious of it now that the Española road has been oiled. Only a few workmen and civilians come this way, to my great relief.

Spring was late in coming but when it did the snow-fed ground burst forth with flowers I had never seen. The juncos, bluebirds, towhees, that fed at the window tray all winter stayed on and many others came. Peas were planted on a cold windy day and the peach blossoms never opened, but there were violets late in March—the first I have persuaded to grow. I fixed a perennial bed near the ace-

quia with plants from Allene's garden and put a table near it under an old apple tree. There Tilano and I ate our lunch on planting days.

On one of those days I crossed the arroyo hoping to find new flowers. Above it on a stony little hill I came suddenly on three Mariposa lilies, the first I had ever seen down here. In the Valle Grande high in the Jemez there are many lavender Mariposas, but here in the valley they are white with golden centers—exquisitely beautiful. There was no contentment then until I had climbed what Hewett calls Mariposa Mesa "where thousands bloom." The old trail was almost gone, but Tilano found a way to the top where I again found three lilies. The seeds must have waited patiently through all these dry years for enough moisture to germinate them.

There on the mesa of old fields but no ruins we found a stone ax and a broken pottery bowl left by some ancient farmer. Why? When? What did he think and feel? These are the things I ponder as I gather sherds—edges, handles, designs all varying as did their makers. I have missed those "ruining" trips during the war, but this year we combined woodgetting and picnics, and so got up on the mesas numerous times. This spot on the river is home and I always return to it eagerly, but it is good to go up to the levels above and look out across the world and back into the past. That is especially true now with the Pueblo boys in France, England, and the Pacific. Slim was wounded soon after D-Day in Normandy but has recovered for more duty. Brownie's ship soon sails. Hilario's destroyer has seen action. Rafael hasn't seen his son for over a year. Sandy feels walled in by the jungle. Two have returned from two years in Alaska and go out to another theatre. I look into the future of their return and adjustment with concern.

In spite of the late spring and strange summer weather, the garden did well. Two of the little boys came to help Tilano and twice a week we sent vegetables up to Los Alamos. The surplus, after house and dinner guests were fed, went into jars and the rootcellar shelves are filled. It was former houseguests who came, understanding the lack of help and willing to have no service. So again there was talk of many things and contact with the outside that I need and enjoy.

The last guest was Peter who came in the fall. Again I climbed

mesas joyfully on non L.A. days and looked at golden trees, forgetting the house. The woodpile grew and the garden harvest was brought in. Wild geese flew south on many days—circling, honking, reforming their silver V to continue on their certain way. The flight of the geese, the deer tracks on the mesas, the first green and the final golden leaves of the cottonwoods, Venus low above the mesa—all these recur.

After Christmas I am going to rest for a month or two, hoping to regain some lost weight. There is a pile of Survey Graphics, Inter-Americans, Foreign Policy bulletins, in addition to a package of books for reading. There will be walks for mail and to the Pueblo to see the new babies. With new batteries there should be music and news. Some evenings Tilano will tell tales of long ago. Seed catalogues will come in and another garden be planted. I look forward to it all.

As the flames of the Christmas Eve fire leap into the night, I shall think of my friends with gratitude and with joy.

III. Christmas 1945

New Year's day of this historic 1945 held no hint of the atomic era. There were no blasts from the Pajarito Plateau making discord in the song of the chorus as I sat in the sun on an old portal at San Ildefonso. Teen, just past two, watched the dancers with me and later demonstrated the steps of the little deer. The only indication of war was the absence of his father and the other young men.

During January I rested and learned to milk, but the Pueblo prepared for San Ildefonso's feast day on the 23rd. It was the time for the ceremonial Buffalo dance and once again I took Tilano over to the house where he and all the dancers would make themselves ready. On the morning of the fourth day they went into the hills before dawn to await the haunting song of the chorus. I leaned against an old adobe house as the deep drum tones rolled and the song called the men who danced as godly animals. For hundreds of years a chorus has called and a line of women waited at the foot of the hill—waited to touch these men and take into themselves

that intangible spiritual power sometimes attained by human beings. As the song reached its climax, a long, grey plumed serpent of smoke rose from the hilltop and spread over the pueblo. From between the hills came the leader, the hunters, the Buffalo lady and men. From over the hills came Deer and Antelope and Mountain Sheep. All came to the foot of the hill where the women waited to touch them, where the chorus waited to accompany them to the plaza with an exultant song.

Tilano, who has always been a Deer, became the leader this year. Babies I had held were grown up enough to be Antelope and Sheep. Tomacita and Facundo were Buffalo and their son slept in his cradle in the ceremonial house while they danced. These human bonds made contact for me, so that the snow falling softly and quietly on the earth, on deer antlers and buffalo manes and curved sheep horns, was significant.

Pruning was finished but the first peas had not been planted when Joe came to tell me that his father, Ignacio, had gone on his last journey to the hills. It was to Ignacio's house that John Boyd had taken me 23 years ago. It was Ignacio who told me, "If, when we dance, our hearts are right, the rain will come." There were many memories as I watched the candles flicker at his side—memories of him and those others who had preceded him. Just the month before, stooped and almost blind, he had served at the mass for Tonita. He had lived a long, full, active life. The moccasins beneath his blanket were well worn. He would have been unhappy sitting by the fire. I miss him as I still miss Juan Estevan and Sayah, but I cannot mourn.

Summer was dry and hot—so hot. I searched in vain for Mariposa lilies in June though the hills had been gay with flowers in May. The weeks seemed an endless round of gathering vegetables and preparing meals. There was tension and accelerated activity on the Hill (Los Alamos) with the men "going south" (to the Alamogordo site). Explosions on the Plateau seemed to increase and then to cease. Men were in the Pacific, leaving wives on the Hill. Things—unknown things—were happening.

The climax came on that August day when the report of the atomic bomb flashed around the world. It seemed fitting that it was

Kitty Oppenheimer who, coming for vegetables, brought the news. I had not known what was being done up there, though in the beginning I had suspected atomic research. Much was now explained. Now I can tell you that Conant and Compton came in through the kitchen door to eat ragout and chocolate cake; that Fermi, Allison, Teller, Parsons came many times; that Oppenheimer was the man I knew in pre-war years and who made it possible for the Hill people to come down; that Hungarians, Swiss, Germans, Italians, Austrians, French and English have been serious and gay around the candlelit table. It has been an incredible experience for a woman who chose to live in a supposedly isolated spot. In no other place could I have had the privilege of knowing Niels Bohr, who is not only a great scientist but a great man. In no other way could I have seen develop a group feeling of responsibility for presenting the facts to the people and urging the only wise course —international control of atomic energy and bombs.

Perhaps the desperate state of the world and the anguish of millions as the constant backdrop of life intensified the joys that fall always brings. This year there were trips to the Plateau for wood on days when sky and aspens vied with each other in beauty. The wind made melody in tall pines while I gathered pine knots, those multi-shaped legacies of long forgotten trees. They seem to be the essence of the elements garnered by a tree and now released in the fireplace to complete the cycle. Their gathering has become as much a part of the fall ceremonies as the garden harvesting and the southward flight of the wild geese. This rhythmic order of nature holds for me assurance as well as beauty.

Perhaps a similar human need is satisfied when people return to this spot and find it unchanged. Los Alamos boys bring wives and babies and hope there is a piece of remembered cake, which has become a symbol. The new Los Alamos people leave, planning to come back. But this is a changing world. Perhaps what they really want is to find the essence unchanged. That becomes my challenge.

And now it is December, with longed-for snow clouds advancing and retreating. Today Tilano and I went for Christmas greens. With ample gas we could go in search of fir and we chose Water Canyon where the old Frijoles road climbed up on the mesa in my

tenderfoot days. Today there were fresh deer and turkey tracks in the road and pieces of fir under a tree brushed by antlers. Snow flurries hit Los Alamos but sun shone on Tsacoma, the sacred mountain of the west.

On this Christmas Eve some of the Pueblo boys will help to light the little fires. Others will be homeward bound. The war is over. Peace is still to be secured. The scientists know that they cannot go back to their laboratories leaving atomic energy in the hands of the armed forces or the statesmen. Nor can I concern myself only with my kitchen, for I, too, am one of the people.

As the pitch wood of the fire releases its stored energy here by the river when Christmas Eve darkens the mesas my thoughts and wishes will go out in all directions to you, my friends.

IV. Christmas 1946

This year really began on the Sunday before Christmas 1945. That day I was taken up to Los Alamos for the first time since the school commencement in June 1941. Falling snow softened outlines of trailer camps, hutments, apartments, barracks, machine shops. Barbed wire secured but did not hide the "Tech Area" where men had worked tensely a few months before to bring into being the atomic bomb. Here a new era had begun, but the normal reaction of excitement was overshadowed by the terrifying possibilities of this new power.

The Pueblo had long looked forward to Christmas, when the boys would be home. Some did come and Rafael realized his dream of two Christmas Eves passed in England to be Santa Claus at the school party. Tall, diffident, wounded Slim, whom the children adore, was home at last and came over here with them for the annual party. I shall never forget that group, from sixth-graders to toddlers, sitting on the floor around the Christmas tree and looking up at Slim as they sang at his request—"Silent Night."

By the time Peter came in February it was evident that problems had been intensified, not solved by war—communal as well as international. Always we hope for a magic touch or word, but human

relationships have to be worked at. Feeling the urgency, we put our minds to work, but minds alone are not sufficient. So we went out into the sunshine and walked beside the river where slender grasses made swaying shadows and tiny animals left miniature tracks on the sand. We looked long at the pattern of a mesa made by the centuries and knew that waiting and believing were essential too.

In the Pueblos old ceremonial dances were being revived. Some I had never seen, others not for years. It was good to see a long line of men and boys dancing with the women bringing baskets of corn-meal and bread to place before them. It was with awe that I watched a sinking Easter sun shine on men's dancing bodies painted yellow and on the spreading eagle feathers of the women's headdress. Soldiers and sailors had returned from Europe and Japan to lay aside uniforms and wear again ceremonial kirtles and moccasins. Could the habits of war be so easily discarded?

Spring came early after a dry winter. Wild geese flew north in February and leaves were unfolding as I pruned the raspberries. Some peach and apricot blossoms defied the calendar and paid the penalty. But no rain came with the spring. The sun blazed and dry winds blew. Plants in the garden struggled to live. Wild flowers that braved the drought soon faded. Grass turned brown and crackled under foot. The Valle Grande, that beautiful green crater high in the Jemez, was brown in June with sheep and cattle only in the narrow strip of green beside the stream. Water was rationed in Santa Fe. Some of us recalled another year of drought when cattle lay dead on the hills—and were fearful. Tree rings had vivid meaning.

Then early in July there was a miracle. Rain came and after only a few short storms the grass was green. Trees held up their leaves. Plants began to grow. Human nerves relaxed. Fears receded as we forgot how helpless we are without rain. When I saw the Valle Grande in September it was luxuriantly green and cattle were fat. Fringed gentians grew beside a stream. The broom grass mesa was a tapestry of red paint brush, many blue and yellow asters, graceful grasses and pine tree shadows.

Summer brought house guests, the vegetable business and can-ning—necessitating an interlude in the Los Alamos dinners. It

brought, too, congenial evenings in the starlight and early mornings in the garden picking raspberries while humming birds whirred and whirled.

After the September Corn dance, opening chamisa buds took up the golden challenge of fall, begun by the smaller wild flowers. Cottonwoods followed until the valley shone. On the lagoon a pair of white egrets and blue herons stood motionless, reflected with the sky in the water. The kingfisher drove away an intruder on his domain. Grosbeaks moved in to noisily eat the bumper crop of juniper berries. It was time to prepare for winter and we went happily up on the Plateau to gather pineknots for the fireplaces. Now, as I recall the feel of warm sunshine, the smell of pine needles, the sound of the wind high in the trees, the peace of the little canyon, I find myself contrasting that fuel-getting with the mining of coal.

Such mental questioning and awareness of the world prompted formation of a small discussion group here in the valley. It is an attempt to increase our share of public opinion by pooling information and clarifying our reactions. Most of us find it an incentive and a mental stimulus. Perhaps, too, it is a beginning of community awareness. We, all Anglos, are newcomers in a valley long inhabited by Spanish-Americans and Indians—a small scale world. My hope is a real community group.

As a balancing factor there is always the fascinating past of the Pajarito Plateau and its people, to whose personality bits of broken pottery and artifacts offer a clue—which seems to have given me a hobby. This fall as I rested on the ruined wall of Navawii I heard a familiar sound. Looking up, my vision finally caught a thin silver V far above the ruin—wild geese southward bound. I had always thought of geese as following the river. Now I knew that some used the Plateau for their high road and that Navawii women must have listened, too, and watched that undulating silver line against the blue fall sky, then hastened their preparation for winter.

Today we gathered the Christmas greens. Large Los Alamos signs bar the canyons where we formerly found fir—even Water Canyon where last year a wild turkey's feather lay beside his tracks. Most of the men whose knowledge made atomic bombs possible

have returned to laboratories and universities to do research, to teach future scientists, to try to solve the world atomic problem. But others have come to continue work on atomic weapons as well as other uses of the energy. So louder and louder blasts echo over the Plateau and my blood runs cold remembering Hiroshima. If the world lived here, all would be reminded frequently that we must catch up with striding science and find a way to live together in the peace that Christmas signifies.

The little wood is ready for the Christmas Eve luminario. As I watch its bright flames and listen to the song of the river, my Christmas wishes will go out across the mesas to you.

V. Christmas 1947

When Tilano lights the little pitch fire on Christmas Eve, those to whom it pays respect will know that human beings now live where last winter only quail, rabbits and coyote made patterns in the snow. The wild geese discovered it when they flew south—some coming very low over the new house. But the blue heron has not followed us from the river to the side of To-tavi-kadi—mesa of the quail. I miss hearing him as he flew homeward after his late supper; miss seeing him standing on one leg in the lagoon as he waited for a minnow to swim across his image in the water. I miss the song of the river, though once I heard it here on a still night. Most of all I miss the rhythmic line of To-tavi against the sky with sunset clouds, a new moon or the evening star above it.

For many the little house at the river was a landmark, for some an experience. For me it was two decades of living and learning. I had hoped to live out my life "where the river makes a noise." The house is still there and surely its walls retain the personality developed through the years from those who came into it, left a little of themselves and went away remembering its simplicity and peace. Each has his own special memory, be it chocolate cake, the scrubbed boards of the kitchen floor, or the Black Mesa framed by a window. For me, at this period, two are especially vivid. I still stand in the kitchen doorway looking into the canyon of the singing river and

up at the two great mesas glistening with snow, dark with rain, everchanging but always steadfast. The other is going into the adobe dining room—darkened against the sun and cool after the kitchen's heat. It was very still and serene and yet alive with the strength of those for whom it had meaning.

When last year's letter went out, I knew that a new bridge would bring the road through the yard very close to the house and that the Los Alamos traffic would be unendurable. Tilano refused to leave, but when I found an open space across the arroyo from the garden, he reconsidered. So when Marie and Adam's family came for supper on Christmas Eve and the children helped to light the pitch fire, I knew that it was the last Christmas by the river.

Sitting here beside the fireplace in Tilano's sunny room with its beautiful view of the mountains, it seems as though a miracle had been performed this year. The months of waiting for a decision about these four acres of Pueblo hillside and the difficulties of building are overshadowed by a truly remarkable manifestation of friendliness. The result is a comfortable house above the arroyo, southeast of the garden and just beneath the basaltic columns where the mesa forms a point. It looks out over the cottonwoods of Tony's fields to the mountains and up the wide arroyo to carved grey mesa points. The mesa to the north towers over it, shutting out the Black Mesa, but giving its own rugged outline. To-tavi shelters it from the southwest wind and reflects the winter sun. Eventually trees will protect from that same reflection in summer. Juniper and a few piñon trees, New Mexican olive and spice bushes, chamisa and cactus, give it a natural garden and spring should bring wild flowers. It is still a very new house but time will blend it with the earth from which it came and give it charm, I hope.

Looking back to those dry windy spring days when I was faced with building a house and a road, finding water, moving stable, corral and chicken houses, I am certain it was a miracle. I had only a few hundred dollars and some old lumber. But Tilano and I had friends—more than we knew. There were those who had found in the guest house rest for weary bodies and minds; those who had watched the morning light move across the mesas and been re-newed. They made possible the beginning and early in May, Tony

Pena came from the Pueblo to make adobe bricks in the garden, where corn grew the year before.

Rain fell on those first adobes but did not damage them. The foundation was laid out in the rain. Tony and Tilano looked happy and said it was good. Now there is snow and Tilano smiles knowingly. There will be grass for the cattle in the spring, water for the fields and perhaps Mariposa lilies. It is probable that the arroyo will have water in it all spring but we can cross it on horseback or in the wagon. No difficulty seems too great when the land has water.

Last May, too, we came in wagons, for there was no road. It was the day of the foundation laying. Facundo and Sandy, Tony and Juanita brought their wagons, and a group from Los Alamos, who had asked to help, worked with them. Men hauled rocks, women fitted them into the trench and mixed mud. Children played in the arroyo water hole and rode in the wagons. It was a good day and I use good as Tilano does when he speaks of rain.

That was just the beginning of many such days—days of hard work in the heat broken by lunch in the meadow. There under the big cottonwoods as they relaxed after lunch, physicists conferred with Tony and Tilano on adobe construction problems. Walls rose and the roof went on—a roof made of old vigas from the Pueblo, new ones from Truchas and Puye, and across them peeled pine saplings covered with roofing paper, mud, more paper and tar, more dirt—a good roof.

When it was time to cover the walls with plaster—first rough, then smooth—the Pueblo people sent word that they wanted to do it. The men mixed the mud and carried it inside to the women. Some kneaded it and handed it to those who, with skilled hands, covered the adobe bricks. There was much talk and laughter and always a beautiful rainbow motion of the hand, so that I look now at the walls and see those plastering days as a rainbow. Old beams were brought for the portal; lumber was found for frames; horses and tools were loaned. More than once I was told "You don't have to pay me. I want to help."

There were also those who gave their interest, advice and belief, like mortar holding bricks together. Most of you knew nothing about this project, but you had faith in what the old house stood for.

It was all of this that gave me courage to clear the many hurdles, as well as appreciation of the fundamental kindness of man.

From this house made from the earth by many hands and hearts, there will go on Christmas Eve to the Pueblo, the Valley, the Hill, on and on across the mesas and mountains, appreciation as warm as the flames from the little fire and the wish that the new house may share its joy with you.

VI. Christmas 1948

The December moon, a silver crescent above the hill to the south, sends my thoughts back a year to the first Christmas in this little house. The little pitch fires blazing up into the twilight of Christmas Eve must have startled the wild creatures whose tracks marked the snow. Tilano and I watched until only embers remained, thinking gratefully of those who had made possible the new house and of all who wished it well.

After the Matachines dance in the Pueblo on Christmas day, Adam brought his family, Maria and Clara, Desideria and Donicio for dinner. The new kitchen was gay with a tiny decorated tree, red candles on the wall, and the long table, as eager-eyed children and laughing grown-ups watched me carve the turkey. If walls take into themselves the scenes they witness, a recording of a happy Christmas must be there in the kitchen's hand-smoothed adobe. As our guests were leaving, the northern mesa stood out so clearly in the moonlight that I was moved to tell Donicio about the eagle I recently had seen circling above the mesa before flying south over To-tavi.

The cough Donicio had that night developed into pneumonia and before New Year's day he had been buried in the church yard. He was the center dancer in a line dance; the chorus grouped itself around him for the Corn Dance; the song seemed to come from him. Now the center was gone—gone like the eagle I again saw flying south on the day he died. Low clouds hung over the Pueblo as we followed his body to the church; at twilight snow fell softly; in the morning the sun shone on a thick white blanket. A deep feeling of loss followed mourning and remained. There were no winter or

spring dances except, on San Ildefonso day, the Comanche dance which is not ceremonial.

In January a succession of storms piled snow upon snow. A hand snow-plough cleared necessary paths and the road. The temperature hovered around fifteen degrees below zero many nights. The wood-pile, neglected during the moving, dwindled fast and we had to bring cottonwood logs from the meadow on the sled. However, we managed to be warm, at least near the fireplace, and to keep well. The road was impassable many days, but fortunately the stable and larder were well-stocked. I worried about Tilano's shoveling so much snow and helped all I could, especially on the roof which had to be done before the walls became wet. Snow and wood kept us busy.

Tilano's room became a winter sitting-room since all day it has sunlight, a wood-conserver. On stormy days I read to him while he tied parrot feathers for the dancers. The radio brought music, news and his favorite programs. On windless days the sun made a sheltered corner beside the kitchen door warm enough for an outdoor tray-lunch, while the dogs played in the snow nearby. Each trip to the woodpile or the chicken yard was into a world where white mesas glistened against a deep blue sky, where snow-covered trees shook starry flakes from their branches. From the wide window near the fireplace we saw storm clouds gather over the mountains or sunset turn the peaks blood red. It was a hard winter, but a good one.

As I watched the geese fly north late in February, I thought apprehensively of all the snow that must reach the river via the arroyo which our road crosses. However, an early thaw, which melted the snow here in the valley, was followed by cold weather so that the run-off from higher levels was gradual. We waded several summer flash floods and rebuilt a short stretch of road, but the arroyo proved itself not the bogey I had feared.

All through the weeks of snow and mud I thought of spring flowers and hoped I would find a Mariposa lily. Before the last ragged snow-patch on the hillside had melted, the sheltered spots were gay with blossoms—pink, lavender and yellow. One day I noticed a slender stalk near the well and watched it hopefully. After a similar winter I had found three Mariposa lilies above the arroyo

and three more high on a mesa. Since then I had looked in vain. Now I waited eagerly for a bud to open and assure me that I had not dreamed an exquisite cream-colored lily with a center of gold. At last the solitary stalk and five more below the house bore blooms, were treasured and remembered as a gift of the snow.

June brought heat, and the Corn Dance in the Pueblo. The people prepared anxiously; for they knew that the chorus had lost its former center and strength. But the day was windless; the dance was good; and they felt, as I did, that Donicio was there, helping both dancers and chorus.

Guests came with summer and the living room couch and a cot on the back porch served as beds. The living room, darkened against the sun, became the cool place where I went for rest and renewal as I had to the adobe dining room of the old house. The portal with its view of the mountains was comfortable by mid-afternoon and there we usually ate supper. Happily we showed many visitors the new house and from the reaction of those who knew the old one I began to feel that the transplanting had been successful, that in time peace might be felt here, too.

The bridge, its superstructure covered with aluminum paint, was finished by mid-summer. The old houses show the wear and tear of many children, with a family in each. Tavi was hit by a truck and no more begs for bones to chase.

In August Adam's family came for a traditional dinner. The tall, slender sailor, who looked at me before he blew out the candles on his nineteenth birthday cake, was Co-ha. Several months earlier he had worn a cap and gown, but always I see him as a baby being christened, a chubby two-year-old calling me "Co-o Warner," a sturdy eight-year-old helping Tilano in the garden.

We were glad to have several families from Los Alamos plant part of the garden this year. It provided escape from the Hill for the men, fun for the children, and renewal for the women, who recognized the special quality of the garden. Lois, who came down frequently to pick vegetables, took the excess up to the Hill and sold it to her friends for us. After the harvest, the men helped Tilano prepare the garden for winter, continuing group work.

With the help of some of the women, I "made a feast" for the

Pueblo in September. About a hundred came in cars and wagons to see the new house and have dinner. I am glad we did it, but I think one family at a time is more satisfactory. Tomacita and Facundo celebrated their tenth wedding anniversary here. Nahn-tu, their son, who has great charm, now shares attention with a beautiful baby sister and Teen, his cousin, goes to school this year.

Fall was especially wonderful with many trips for wood when I again heard the wind in the pines and gathered pineknots for warmth and the good of my soul. Near a ruin we found a trail worn deep in the rock and a woman's thumbprint still visible on a sherd of her pottery. Once while the men chopped wood beside the new wide road on the Plateau, I walked along a mesa until I no longer heard the traffic. There alone in the sunlight I began to understand that nothing man may do, not even the atomic bomb, can in any way touch or change the essence of this country.

Perhaps when Tilano lights the little pitch fire on this Christmas Eve the deer, whose tracks he saw at the foot of the hill, will pause and watch the flames carry up into the night and across the continent our Christmas wish for peace and beauty.

VII. Christmas 1949

Gayly wrapped jars of jam ready for the Christmas Eve trip to the Pueblo remind me that despite mountains marked with only faint lines of snow and cottonwoods still covered with dry bronze leaves, it is the season for translation of this year's living into words.

Last Christmas Eve as I waited in the dusk for the outdoor rehearsal of the Matachines dance, two little boys climbed into the truck with me and in high clear voices sang carols until the fires in front of each house were lighted. Later when Tilano and I left the Pueblo, embers glowed around the plazas and the cold air was pungent with smoke. As we passed the old house, we signalled the children there and by the time we reached home, their two little fires were blazing in the darkness. Tilano quickly lit the two he had laid and as we watched the flames against the dark mesa, we

seemed part of the great circle—a Christmas circle of candles in windows, little fires in the night, hearts gladdened by sharing.

Two years of sun and snow have weathered the new house and rooted it deeply on the side of the sheltering mesa. Some of the problems created by the change have been solved. The yield of garden, cow, chickens, kitchen in the form of bread and jam, supplemented by two annual houseguests, has provided a living. This would be impossible without the friends who devote time and energy to delivery. Also it depends somewhat upon the vagaries of the weather, the insect world, and the creatures themselves. However, any meagerness of return is offset by the lack of strain and the increased leisure to enjoy our surroundings and people. Fortunately our needs are simple and are well supplied with a woodpile, alfalfa for Topsy, and a larder stocked against storms.

It is true that my primary concern two years ago was a place where Tilano could live out his span happily, since without him the twenty years at the bridge would have been impossible. So his room was planned first and as he wanted it. But the house—this house built by many—could not be justified for us alone. It was essential that it have meaning for others. How was it possible to develop quickly that which at the old house had grown slowly and unplanned over a long period of years? How could it be shared when no commercial reason drew people? For these problems there were no established methods. It was not a picture to be painted, a poem to be written. It was not even mine to create. So I lived each day as it presented itself and hoped I would find the way. During my thinking of this summary for you, it has become clear. Perhaps I can make you see how the growing spirit of this house is compounded of the earth itself and the seasons, of daily living, and in great measure of the people who come to it. For they have come.

When I go to feed the chickens each morning, my eyes make the circle of the compass, beginning with the basaltic point of Totavi in the west. Memory supplies its long line above the river, the quiet place on its side where I go to be alone, a tiny crescent ruin covered with dry grasses that shine in the sun, and across the river the carved face of Shumo, whose northern point is visible. Beyond

the valley rise the mountains with Lake Peak sharply outlined against the sky and in the north, T'omo like a great, outstretched prehistoric creature above the road to Los Alamos. These deeply rooted, steadfast mesas provide a bulwark for living in this age, and at the same time present beauty everchanging in color and aspect. On their sides and high places are ceremonial trails and shrines where for centuries men have placed prayer plumes when their hearts were right. Closer and more intimate is the hillside with its old trail, where I have found stones carried long ago in a buckskin pouch. From it the quail come down near the house and a rabbit who nibbles grass unafraid. Above it the crescent winter moon shines and this month Venus is the evening star.

I am glad that the first winter was one of storm and cold, because it necessitated spending many more hours indoors. Tilano's room with its fireplace and sunlight on clear days, quickly became the lived-in center of the house. Here hang his dance costume—buckskin leggings, foxskin, bells—and pictures of the children who call him uncle. Here feathers are sorted and tied with care for the dancers; a headdress or bow and arrows are made for some child; and from his chair he watches in unceasing wonder the cars going to and from Los Alamos. Sometimes there are guests for tea as color follows color from foothills to sky. Sometimes on winter evenings there are tales of long ago. From here he went, when it was time to prepare for the Buffalo dance, to the Pueblo, and returned with the quality of those days spent apart still about him.

The life cycle reaches the house, too, with Brownie inviting us to his wedding, Sandy unable to hide his happiness at the birth of a son. And inevitably there is word of death—of little Oma-peen, of Susana, my friend of many years, of John Boyd who first took me to San Ildefonso. It was he who told me Indian lore, taught me to watch for tracks on the trail, showed me the significance a stone might have. He never saw this house but his influence is here.

One evening as I washed dishes, the sound of a long story in Tewa reached me from Tilano's room. When I went in later, Sandy was sitting where he could hear every word and see every expression and Tilano, looking up with his face aglow, explained, "I am telling Sandy about the Shalako." This year his great desire to see

the Shalako at Zuni has been fulfilled and he relives the experience with each eager listener.

I wish you might see the big kitchen on some Sundays, on Thanksgiving, during Christmas week, on many a day throughout the year. Sometimes it is little blonde children, sometimes black-haired children who run into the kitchen for a drink of water or the basket of toys, go with Tilano to gather the eggs or milk the cow. A car may come from Santa Fe, the Hill, or across the valley with someone who needs to sit awhile here and look at the mountains or the hillside. Rosanita came to celebrate her graduation as a nurse. Louis and Juanita their wedding anniversary. Hagi, who used to help in the garden as a little boy and who hauled all the water for the house-building came with his parents after graduation to discuss his future. Several months later he returned in a Marine uniform to tell us "all about it" and how often he thought of his uncle. Peter and Earle bring weeks of merriment and talk. All year our friends and friends of theirs drive across the arroyo to see how we fare, to look at the mountains, to add a bit of themselves to the spirit of the house.

Rain and snow have come to the dry earth since I began to write and there may be a white hillside as a background for the Christmas Eve fire. We shall watch it and the star above it while we wish you joy—joy in many little things throughout the year.

VIII. Christmas 1950

Tilano is making a feather headdress, bows and arrows, tiny doll moccasins with silver buttons, for the boys and girls to whom he is a special friend. We have gathered the pitch wood for the little fires; and soon you will be expecting this record of the year from the house on the side of the mesa.

As I sit beside the fireplace and think back across the months, I realize that during the whole year my eyes have been scanning the sky for clouds, as now. On San Ildefonso day, January 23, I napped on the ground in a sunny spot. In February we disheartedly put away the snow plow. On Easter the wind blew stinging sand in the faces of the Buffalo dancers all day long. Trees blossomed early and the newly formed fruit buds froze in May. Twentienth Century Fox filmed Two Flags West at San Ildefonso and cursed the wind-blown dust. Water in the irrigation ditch ran slowly day and night while the early corn and beans dried up in the June heat. Early in July the spell seemed broken by a pouring rain that gladdened our hearts and found every hole in powder-dry flat roofs; but in no time the earth was dry again. The Navahos had the clouds seeded for rain while they hauled water for their sheep; and one of their old medicine men journeyed to the four sacred mountains to perform a ceremony for rain. Clouds darkened the western sky and showers fell on the Plateau, sometimes fell with such force that the arroyo, dry all spring, became a rushing torrent. Here in the valley the sun shone as we watched the water wash out the road and fill the garden ditch with gravel. What was left of the garden and our jumpy nerves was saved by the lower temperatures of this strange summer in which the tomatoes were better than ever before. Late one September day Tilano glanced at a dark cloud appearing over the mesa and decided to milk early. Before he had finished, the cloud shed all its hail and rain, which poured off the mesa like waterfalls to make new arroyos and deepen old ones, and wash the mud plaster off the house and under the doors and windows. Since then we can count the drops that have fallen. Carrots were dug with a pick and we have

not tried to plough. Day after day we sit in the sun while every bit of moisture evaporates.

I keep thinking of those prehistoric people who left the Plateau during a long drought, left the pueblos where we find potsherds and arrowpoints in the rubble. They, too, must have scanned the sky with hope and finally with despair before they decided to leave their homes and sacred places to journey to the south. As the Pueblo tale of their ancestors goes, the lazy ones stayed beside the river and made a new home here in the valley. Were they really lazy or did they have faith that their ceremonies still had power to bring the rains again? Always, even in the driest times, Tilano shakes his head emphatically and says, "He has to come."

Tilano, who is about eighty, seems younger this year and very well. With such a small garden, the summer was not strenuous, save for fixing the road each time the arroyo ran, and there have been no special worries until the recent Korean news. If he can work slowly in his own routine and be free from worry, he still can accomplish a great deal. In the evening he relaxes in his easy chair while he listens to the radio or a favorite book. Almost every day brings someone from far or near to see us, so that he is not lonely. For this I am especially glad since I have not been very well and thus not too companionable. However, rest and diet are bound to bring me back to normal and mesa-climbing soon.

Co-ha and Hagi, the boys who worked with Tilano in the garden from the time they could pull a weed, came home on leave before going overseas. We had the traditional family dinners with a chocolate cake for the boy to cut, but this time the gaiety was only on the surface. Five of the boys from the Pueblo have gone and again, after so short a span, the postman is awaited anxiously. But always the cycle moves on and now the youngest boy in that family comes with his cousin to spend the day, to follow Tilano around and to love him.

Several days have passed—days of cloud and of snow above our level. Now the sky is clearing and the clouds in the east have dropped just below the Truchas peaks, which glisten in the sun.

I am sure that I know how the hearts of those long-ago people lightened and with what gratitude they thanked their gods.

How to endure the man-made devastating period in which we live and which seems almost as hopeless to control as drought; how to proceed when leadership seems utterly lacking, when individuals and nations seem stupid and arrogant; these no one human can answer. I only know that the power recognized by those other sky-scanners still exists, that contact is possible. I know, too, what depths of kindness and selflessness exist in my fellow man. Of this I have had renewed assurance recently, when those about me have shared self and substance.

When Tilano lights the Christmas Eve fire, perhaps against a white hillside, I shall watch from the house where some have felt peace and hope that in your sky there are some bright stars.

January 26, 1951, Dorothy McKibbin to Peggy Church

Dear Peggy

Edith Warner had an operation yesterday which proved to be unsuccessful and her sister Vel and the doctors do not expect her to live very long. She is in the Illinois Masonic Hospital in Chicago. Her sister asks that if anyone writes they make it cheerful and hopeful so that Edith won't have any more worry than necessary.

I thought you would like to know about her. . . .

Love
Dorothy

May 1951, from Vel Ludlow

Dear Friends of Edith Warner

On March 27th Edith left the hospital at Los Alamos to return to her home with a nurse to care for her. During the days which followed, she wrote this message to all of you:

"After weeks in a hospital, it is especially wonderful to be here in Tilano's room—which is the winter living room. Here he can rub my arm to relax me and give me of his calm and strength. From the bed I can see the first light on the mountains, watch the snow clouds rise from the

glistening Truchas peaks, follow the sunset color from the valley to the sky. I can feel the mesas even though I do not see them and almost hear the song of the river. It is a good place in which to wait for the passing from a rich full life into whatever work lies beyond. You, my many friends, have contributed so much to the fullness of my life through the years and in the past months have given of your thoughts and prayers, as well as more material assistance.

Whatever you may have felt here of peace and stillness came from the great Source of life and will be here always. I was but a channel, for which I am most grateful.

Since I cannot be well to take care of Tilano, I am happy and at peace. I would have you think of me that way."

During those weeks she saw many friends and had an opportunity to exchange thoughts and feelings often left unsaid. She felt it was a wonderful experience and that she had been unusually blessed.

On May 4th Edith passed into "immortal summer."

Peggy Pond Church wrote this poem for Edith who wanted you to share it with her.

REQUIEM FOR EDITH

It is hard to say what you have been to us,
as though while time foamed like a sea, while the floods rose
  around us,
yours was the window that showed always the tranquil candle,
the house by the side of the road, the tender welcome,
the comfortable stove, good talk in winter,
and you, the listening one whose silence healed us.
When you have gone, where shall we turn for blessing?
Who will speak to us of the beauty of mountain and mesa?
Who will listen for us to the unspoken wisdom
of morning and evening and the changing seasons?

Oh you, whose roots were so deep in a time of uprooting,
how can our restless spirits find rest? Live now within us
like a spring of clear water. Be present in your garden
like a gentle ghost. Let us often find you
there under the drowsy shadow of ancient apple
where the green lettuce sprouts, and old Tilano
kneels still to coax the water among the long rows
of ripening berry. Tell us you have forgotten
the long anguish of dying, that it was after all only the seed
splitting from its hard shell, and against all of earth's weight,
bursting at last into light and immortal summer.

DRAWINGS BY CONNIE FOX BOYD

THE UNIVERSITY OF NEW MEXICO PRESS

THE HOUSE AT OTOWI BRIDGE